Above: *Father Chaminade's signature: The "G" stands for Guillaume (William), his given name. He preferred to use his Confirmation name, Joseph. Chaminade's birth-death dates are April 8, 1761 - January 22, 1850.*

A Half-Century On Kalaepohaku
Chaminade University 1955-2005

VITA IN VERBO

Chaminade University

1955 | 2005

The First Marianist

Born in Perigueux, France, some 60 miles northeast of Bordeaux, William Chaminade (he preferred his Confirmation name, Joseph) went at the age of ten to the College of Mussidan, where one of his brothers was a professor.

First as a student, then as teacher, steward, and chaplain, he remained at the college 20 years. As the violence of the French Revolution spread through the countryside, Chaminade was first forced to disguise himself and minister in hiding, and later fled Bordeaux at the risk of falling victim to the guillotine. During this dangerous period he met Marie Therese Charlotte de Lamorous who was working with lay women. She and Chaminade remained advisors to one another for 40 years and offered each other spiritual, economic, and administrative support. She was instrumental in establishing Chaminade's many Sodalities, beginning in 1801.

Some priests—called Constitutional clergy—took the schismatic oath of allegiance to the revolutionary government, while others, like Father Chaminade, opposed the new government from hiding or in exile. Taking refuge in Spain, Fr. Chaminade spent three years in Saragossa ministering to thousands of other exiles and praying at the shrine of Our Lady of the Pillar where he envisioned new ways for dealing with the crisis of faith in France. Father Chaminade returned to France, believing that the rebuilding of the Church in the aftermath of the Revolution would best be accomplished by engaging the laity in small communities of faith, dedicated to prayer, education, and acts of service to the larger community.

In 1808 Chaminade began to correspond with Adele de Batz de Trenquellon, who had established a rural network of women. This group complemented and extended the goal of rechristianizing society through spiritual support and an apostolic approach. The various groups of all three founders were open to all Christians, of all classes and both sexes who were dedicated to good works and

Blessed Father William Joseph Chaminade

spiritual progress. They were strengthened by the horrors of the Revolution and these tests of faith and determination resulted in a firm foundation of followers. They were able to "start fresh" with a mission that was both idealistic and practical. After two decades of work, and the founding of the Daughters of Mary in 1816, the third part of his vision of the Marianist Family materialized when he founded the Society of Mary, a religious community of priests and lay brothers in 1817. Laity—women in particular—reserved and passed on the teachings of Christianity. They formed a network of support for priests who refused to take the civil oath by ministering to the faithful and providing moral encouragement.

Within the ruinous social environment left by the upheaval, Father Chaminade began meeting with lay men and women to preserve and share their faith, building new communities of believers. Inspired by the example of Mary, who embodied the attributes of the gospel, Chaminade's growing movement spread throughout a bewildered and hungry France. He wrote of this Marianist movement, "The spirit of faith will become a spirit of confidence in God, a spirit of zeal and a spirit of courage and generosity."

Central to Father Chaminade's legacy is his commitment to forming schools as a principal means for transforming society. Marianist schools are communities concerned with the education of the whole person, respecting both faith and reason as means to the truth, and preparing graduates for success in their careers and lives. In 1849, members of the Society of Mary (Marianists) came to the United States to minister to immigrant populations. They founded first what is now the University of Dayton and, shortly after, what became St. Mary's University of San Antonio, Texas. In 1883 eight Marianists arrived in Honolulu, five of whom assumed leadership of what is now Saint Louis School. Today the Society of Mary serves over 100 schools in 30 countries. Chaminade University of Honolulu is named for Father Chaminade, who was beatified in 2000 by Pope John Paul II.

A Half-Century On Kalaepohaku
Chaminade University 1955-2005

Brother Jerry Bommer, S.M. • Linda M. Iwamoto • MacKinnon Simpson

Chaminade, Alma Mater, Hail!

Light of truth by tropic sea,
Guide of youth, you keep us free.
Your colors: white as curling foam,
Your royal blue - our island home.
Lift our loyal spirits high,
With a sword of inspiration
Lead to battle with the cry,
"Life in the word" - and victory
For love of God and nation.
Rendezvous of West and East
Home of evening star, a gleam,
And morning star, pure silver beam,
Hail, splendor, echo of the sun.
Lift our loyal spirits high,
With the sword of inspiration
Lead to battle with the cry,
"Life in the word" - and victory
                    Bro. Joseph Becker, S.M.

PUBLISHER:

Chaminade University
3140 Waialae Avenue
Honolulu, Hawai'i 96816-1578
(808) 735-4711
www.chaminade.edu

Library of Congress Catalog
Card Number 2005906977
ISBN:0-9706213-3-7
Hard cover trade edition
Printed in China
First trade edition, August 2005

Dedication

This book is dedicated to the Chaminade *'ohana*—students, alumni, faculty, staff, administrators, donors, and all who have contributed to the vision and mission. As Chaminade strides into its second half-century, we pause to reflect on the first fifty years. It has been a time of determination, of challenges, and of astonishing achievements. From a tiny junior college in classrooms borrowed from St. Louis High School to a fine university just fifty years later, the climb has been as steep as the hill on which the institution sits. This book is the story of that climb.

TOM PATTERSON • PATTERSON GRAPHICS

Above: *The entrance sign on Waialae Avenue was erected in 1979 with a $1000 donation from Chaminade student James E. Smalec, a three-tour Vietnam veteran.*

TABLE OF CONTENTS

ST. LOUIS COLLEGE

—NUUANU RIVER—
HONOLULU, H.I.

—B.BERTRAM—

CHAPTER I

The Beginnings of Saint Louis College

One of the very earliest schools in the Islands, Saint Louis was founded in 1846 on a 216-acre grant of land from King Kamehameha III at ʻAhuimanu on Windward Oʻahu near Kaneʻohe. Reflecting its verdant location, the original name was College of ʻAhuimanu (which in Hawaiian means "cluster of birds.") The first school was administered by the Fathers of the Sacred Hearts of Jesus and Mary. Classes were taught in Hawaiian until 1859 when English was substituted.

By 1880 the school had moved over the Koʻolau to downtown Honolulu. It had outgrown its campus, and perhaps more importantly, there was a huge population shift from outlying districts to the expanding city. The newly arrived secular priest Father William J. Larkin raised $10,000 and purchased 2 acres of land on the mauka side of Beretania Street, adjoining Washington Place, home of John Dominis, Governor of Oʻahu, and his wife, Princess Liliʻuokalani. On the property stood "Stonehouse," a former residence constructed of large coral blocks; here Larkin became principal of St. Louis College which began under the name, "College of St. Louis, an Hawaiian Commercial and Business Academy," most likely named for the patron saint of Honolulu's Bishop Louis Maigret. The proposed curriculum was ambitious, including Latin, Greek, French, German, Spanish, Italian, history, geography, mathematics, physics, chemistry, and commercial studies. The school began with 28 students and 3 instructors.

However, Larkin was not to carry through due to a tragic architectural accident. A large hall was erected, but the walls soon started to bulge ominously. Two long steel reinforcing rods were placed to stabilize it, but

*Facing Page: Saint Louis College campus along Nuʻuanu Stream photographed by Brother Bertram. **Inset:** An early St. Louis College football team. According to Brother Joe Becker, "Athletics have always been a favorite activity at St. Louis ..."*

they snapped suddenly on May 20, 1881, and the edifice collapsed, killing a young Hawaiian boy, David Paaho. The accident was blamed on faulty design, and both the architect and Larkin were held responsible. With Larkin in jail awaiting trial for second degree manslaughter, the school stumbled along for another year. Although Fr. Larkin wished to stand trial, he was advised to leave the country.

In 1883, the Bishop of Honolulu bought 4 acres of land on the ʻEwa bank of Nuʻuanu Stream. Just sixty-six years after French priest Father William Joseph Chaminade founded the Society of Mary—eight Brothers clambered down the gangplank of the steamship *S.S. Mariposa* to a wharf in Honolulu Harbor. Three soon departed for St. Anthony's on Maui, and the remaining five had been assigned to organize the fledgling St. Louis College. Those five men were led by Brother Bertram Gabriel Bellinghausen, who assumed leadership of the school. Bro. Bertram, immortalized as the namesake of Bertram Street on St. Louis Heights, had a hobby—photography—and he was the equal of many professionals. He set out to document the Islands, and his images of the era which have survived are exquisite.

On December 12, 1899, bubonic plague was discovered in Honolulu's Chinatown, right across Nuʻuanu Stream from the school. No one at the time understood how the so-called "Black Death" spread, and Chinatown was immediately placed under strict quarantine enforced by armed troops. Eventually the Board of Health decided to burn down any building where a plague victim had been found. These planned blazes were set and controlled by the Honolulu Fire Department, and the process had been flawless until the Saturday morning of January 20, 1900.

A fire was set around noon and was kept well under control until a sudden wind whipped glowing embers up to one of the twin steeples of the large Protestant Kaumakapili Church on Beretania Street which had a

Above: *The decrepit residence of the Brothers at 'Ahuimanu, with Ko'olau cliffs in back, taken in 1926. By this time the school had moved twice already and was poised for a third move to Kalaepohaku.*

Above: *"Stonehouse" next to Washington Place was the building occupied by Saint Louis College after moving from the windward side.*

primarily Hawaiian congregation. The steeples were too high for the Fire Department's strongest pumper to reach.

Bro. Bertram was at the school when the blaze began to rage out of control. Setting up his view camera (likely on the second floor *lanai* of the Boarder's Building), he snapped a series of twenty-eight glass-plate shots that chronicled the destruction of the Kaumakapili Church, and the ensuing inferno that also claimed thirty-eight acres of Chinatown.

The school spent its next forty-five years on the downtown campus across from River Street. Today the short street named College Walk is the only vestige of almost a half century of education there.

By the 1920s it was clear that more space was needed, and a search was initiated to find a new campus. The electric streetcars of Honolulu Rapid Transit snaked around the city providing transportation for day students, and it was important to locate any new facilities close to the line. (Some two decades earlier, when moving their own cramped campus from downtown, Mid-Pacific Institute had chosen land in Manoa Valley over Palolo in part because of its convenient streetcar access.)

The Brothers found Kalaepohaku [stone promontory], an empty 204-acre parcel of rocky hillside along the streetcar tracks on Wai'alae Avenue in Kaimuki. It formed the highland between Manoa and Palolo valleys. They purchased the property from Bishop Estate in 1923. Unfortunately the rushing waters of Palolo Stream traversed a deep gully right at streetside of the property, restricting convenient access until a large concrete culvert could be installed and a roadway across it and on to campus could be built.

For several years steamshovels clanked and crunched across the lava and *panini* [cactus] while preparing the hillside for the new school. Selecting a building site high up the hill, a circular driveway was laid and four substantial structures—Bertram, Freitas, Henry and Eiben Halls—were constructed and finished as classroom and residential facilities.

In 1928 the school moved from River Street to the beautiful new campus. June 7 marked the first official event at Kalaepohaku—commencement for the class of 1928 in Bertram Hall. That fall the campus was dedicated and classes began.

Bertram Gabriel Bellinghausen, S.M.—Brother, Principal and Shutterbug

Brother Bertram

Like many of the early Marianists who served in Hawai'i, Bro. Bertram was European, born in Germany. He was dedicated, authoritarian, and a stickler for details. Discipline and school spirit were both high, and the education was superb. A fine violinist, he conducted the student band for many years. He was a close friend of King David Kalakaua, and the monarch often appeared at school functions.

Brother Bertram left St. Louis in 1905, after 21 years as the school's director. During his term he had increased the student body from 75 to 700. He left behind hundreds of well-educated students and a priceless collection of historic photographs.

Above: *In 1889 Brother Bertram shot the then-new OR&L Main Depot at Iwilei (replaced many years later by the current structure).*

Above: *Under orders from the Board of Health, ramshackle buildings near Kaumakapili Church were scheduled to be torched by the fire department in order to destroy the plague virus. On January 20, 1900, all four HFD engines were on hand to control the blaze and protect the church, but a sudden wind swirled embers high on to one of the twin steeples. It ignited in flame, too high for the Fire Department to extinguish. Here, Brother Bertram has captured one steeple already collapsed and the roof ablaze. The fire roared out of control and by day's end, thirty-eight acres of Chinatown were destroyed. Once the riverfront buildings caught fire, Bro. Bertram's camera perch must have been hot indeed.*

Inset: *After the fire, Chinatown was surrounded by a high fence as it all had to be resurveyed. Bro. Bertram gained access and took this stark photo of the skeleton of Kaumakapili Church amidst the devastation of what had been— a few days before—a vibrant neighborhood.*

CHAPTER II

Kalaepohaku

As befits its name, which translates to "stone promontory," the hillside purchased for the school was steep, rocky, and dry. Sale of the property closed in 1923; a bridge accessing the land was built over Palolo Stream in 1925 allowing surveying and road construction to begin. Brother Adolph Eiben organized the effort, and St. Louis College opened for classes in the fall of 1928 with 1200 students and 51 Brothers in attendance.

The original buildings, all still in use, were Bertram, Freitas, Henry and Eiben. A need was felt almost immediately for a science building (now Newel) and eighty acres were sold for house lots on what became St. Louis Heights, with streets named for early Brothers: Robert, Frank, Herman, Eugene, Alphonse, Felix, Bertram.

The school prospered in Kaimuki, at least for its first 4977 days of operation. Then at midnight December 7, 1941, with fires still raging at Pearl Harbor and nervous, trigger-happy troops awaiting an expected invasion, all Island schools—public, private and parochial—were closed indefinitely. St. Louis was impacted more than most, as some eight months earlier, the Army had arranged to lease the campus in the event of war. By dawn on December 8, Brothers, boarders and volunteers began moving desks and other school paraphenalia out and truckloads of hospital equipment in. Henry Chapel (now Sullivan Library) became a surgical ward, and the science labs in Newel became research and testing labs. Over the course of the war, some 78 temporary structures were built by the Army. Bertram Hall became an operating theatre. A hastily-stenciled sign on Waiʻalae Avenue now read "Provisional General Hospital No. 2," a designation changed on July 1 to "147th General Hospital." Students were replaced by patients,

Facing Page: *Four views of Kalaepohaku and Palolo Stream before construction began. Waialae Avenue crosses the middle of the photo at top left.*

teachers and administrators by doctors and nurses. Some 33,000 patients passed through the 2,500-bed facility, and the Army's $90,000 annual rent liquidated the school's heavy debt assumed during construction in 1928.

Some seven weeks after the surprise attack, with the elementary boys safely ensconced at St. Patrick's, classes resumed for the older students at McKinley High School, in an arrangement with that school's principal Dr. Miles Carey. McKinley's own students filled the classrooms for four hours in the morning, and the St. Louis boys occupied them for four hours in the afternoon. The St. Louis class of 1945 has long differentiated itself as the one which graduated after four years without attending its own school.

Perhaps the most exciting wartime event on campus was the August 1944 arrival of a Packard convertible bearing President Franklin Delano Roosevelt, coming to visit wounded soldiers recovering at the hospital after evacuation from the front lines of the Pacific War.

After the war the school's buildings were restored to their prewar functions. The school also purchased fourteen of the buildings constructed by the Army, including a 600-seat auditorium and barracks to be used as dorms for boarders and Brothers. On January 26, 1946, about five months after V-J Day, the Army presented a symbolic key to the facilities to Brother Leo Rautsch, and the Kalaepohaku campus reopened for classes.

World War II produced more than restored buildings, aerial aces, Jeeps, Liberty ships, and victory on two fronts. It also produced the G.I. Bill of Rights so that those millions who served their nation were eligible for a free college education.

The subject of creating a Marianist institution of higher education in Hawaiʻi had been first proposed in 1938. After the war, it was again presented to the Marianist authorities in Dayton, Ohio. It would be nine years— 1955—until five young Marianists were called to found a junior college.

A Saint Louis College Album

Above: *Aerial view of proposed St. Louis campus from offshore Waikiki. The Moana Hotel is at bottom left.*

Above: *Aerial photo c.1929. Buildings (with current names) counterclockwise from upper left: Newel Hall, Bertram Hall, Freitas Hall, Henry Hall, Eiben Hall.*

Above: *Members of the 1929 Sophomore Improvement Club pose with their shovels and wheelbarrow.*

Above: *Boulders were everywhere and excavation was a laborious process. Early steamshovels were powered by steam boilers.*

Above: *Moving Day from the old Nuʻuanu Stream campus up to Kalaepohaku in Kaimuki.*

Above: *On September 17, 1929, a fire started in the Henry Hall locker room during football practice. The players helped firefighters extinguish the blaze. Bro. Eiben is dressed in black at upper left.*

Above: *St. Louis College logo above Freitas doorway.*

Above: *St. Louis students forming an honor guard to welcome The Very Reverend Walter Tredtin in 1939.*

Above: *Seniors working in the oval in 1930.*

Above: *Digging holes for the banyan trees*

Above: *Moving dirt from Palolo Stream up to the oval in a Model T Ford truck.*

Above: *At hard labor.*

SLC School Days

Above: *Babe Ruth on the Freitas Hall steps in 1933. The NY Yankees had stopped here on their way to a barnstorming tour in Japan. Raised by Brothers in a Catholic orphanage in Maryland, Ruth ofter visited parochial schools.*

Above: *Organized by Bro. Bertram in 1907, the St. Louis Alumni Association first met in a downtown building donated by August Dreier. In 1937 the Association purchased this Isenberg Street building, which they named Dreier Manor in his honor. Torn down after a 1950 fire, the present SLAA clubhouse was erected on the site.*

Above: *Bro. James Wipfield in his Henry classsroom in 1938. He arrived in1929 and stayed some two decades. Many of these historic photos are his.*

Above: *1931 Junior Police Picnic on Kailua Beach.*

Above: *Cast of the SLC Commercial Club play:* She Is A He, *presented Christmas 1934.*

Above: *SLC star Bill "The Knee" Pacheco.*

The Wartime Years

Above: *During his July 1944 visit to Oʻahu, President Franklin D. Roosevelt came on campus to encourage troops recuperating in the Army Hospital.*

Above: *Henry's arches and doorways were converted to use blackout curtains at night.*

Above: *A spiderweb of ramps connecting barracks.*

Above: *On July 1, 1942, 500 medical personnel arrived and many were housed in these platform tents.*

147TH GENERAL HOSPITAL

Above: *Maj. Clara Raven, MD was Chief of the 147th Laboratory Services. She was one of the first five women physicians permitted to join the Army.*

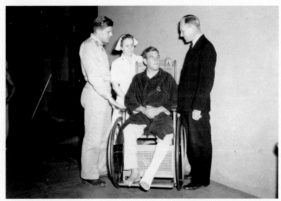

Above: *On February 6, 1942 Pfc. Robert Hungate poses with hospital chief Major J.P. Bachman, Army nurse Lt. Ione Featherston, and St. Louis president Brother Paul Sibbing.*

Above: *Brothers in a "Hilo Sampan." Note ramps at right and over road.*

Above: *A covered wooden ramp on campus.*

Above: *First section of Army Mess Hall from Green Valley Jungle Training Camp being moved to the Brothers' retreat in Punaluʻu. Second and third from left: Bro. August Kretschmer, Joe Kalili.*

CHAPTER III

Chaminade

According to Father Stephen Tutas, one of the five founders of Chaminade, the need for a Catholic liberal arts college in Hawai'i was first felt in the late 1930s. Like everything else in the Islands, plans were disrupted by the ensuing war, and the college wasn't actually created until ten years after war's end, when the first class of thirty students enrolled. It was a small but vital start, and during the next half century, Chaminade awarded more than 17,200 degrees.

Evolution of the institution's name took place over a 22-year period. It was founded as St. Louis Junior College. Since the high school with which it shares the campus had historically been called St. Louis College, that itself was confusing. In 1957 the school became co-educational, expanded to a four-year curriculum, and changed its name to Chaminade College in honor of Marianist founder Father William Joseph Chaminade. In 1977 a graduate program was added, and the name was changed yet again to become Chaminade University of Honolulu.

The St. Louis Alumni Association had been especially determined that Marianists create a facility of higher education. Bro. Joe Becker wrote in *New Wars,* "To gauge the pulse of the Catholic population more accurately, St. Louis College sent a questionnaire to all schools under Catholic auspices. Ninety percent favored founding a university under the direction of the Brothers of Mary and 85 percent were willing to contribute to a drive for funds."

A search was started for a campus elsewhere in Honolulu, but the cost to buy land and create an infrastructure was too great so the new institution would share Kalaepohaku with St. Louis. It was a proven site, easy to access,

with available land and with facilities—classrooms, dormitories, and food services—already in operation. Best of all, the crushing debt had been paid off by leasing the campus to the Army during World War II.

Yet starting a college from scratch was still a daring and expensive proposition and while the five men selected as founders had great faith and energy, none had any experience in such a daunting task. With thirty students that first September semester, and four classrooms in Henry Hall, they struggled forward, under the leadership of Father Robert Mackey, S.M., worrying over every dime and every dollar.

Chaminade later became the first private college in Honolulu to offer evening adult learning programs and the first degree-granting institution to offer course work on military bases. Chaminade has also been a pioneer in online learning, beginning in 1995. Over 60 online courses in 15 disciplines give students an opportunity to earn a degree from anywhere in the world.

Ironically, despite educating thousands of students over the past half-century, Chaminade's worldwide acclaim rests on a couple of hours in 1982 when the underdog basketball team scored a 77-72 victory over the then-number-one ranked University of Virginia starring Ralph Sampson, still regarded as the biggest upset in the history of college basketball.

In 1995, Dr. Mary Civille Wesselkamper became Chaminade's eighth president and the first woman to serve in such a post in Hawai'i's history. With 22 degree programs of study, six master's degree programs, a variety of professional certificate programs, and strong off-campus and online programs, Chaminade offers an excellent Catholic liberal arts education, and has graduates from every U.S. state and 45 countries around the world.

Chaminade University continues the tradition of Father Chaminade in educating for the heart, mind and soul.

Facing Page: *Rising to the occasion. Workman prepare the site for a statue of Father Chaminade.*

The Five Founders

In 1883 five enthusiastic Marianists took over operation of St. Louis College. And in 1955 five enthusiastic Marianists founded Chaminade. Thirty students awaited them, all young men, although that would soon change. The institution was founded as a two-year junior college, and that would soon change as well.

The move to create a Marianist institution of higher learning in the Islands had been floated for decades, and might have come to fruition earlier had not the bombs raining on Pearl Harbor on Dcember 7, 1941 changed everything. After the war, there was a spirit that anything was do-able.

The G.I. Bill, offering a college education to every one of the millions who served in uniform in WWII, meant that the University of Hawai'i was bulging at the seams. Some 600 applicants each year were being refused admission for lack of space. It was time.

Reflecting on the founding and first fifty years of Chaminade, co-founder Fr. Steven Tutas recently remarked, "It went fast...it all seems like yesterday." Father Tutas, the youngest of the five co-founders, recalls that the core group had to be versatile and adaptable. "We did everything." He, for instance, was school chaplain, taught theology, philosophy, psychology, French, and served as assistant janitor. "The head janitor," he recalls, "was the president, Father Mackey."

After the very first year, the school had to re-organize when the Dean and history instructor, Bro. John McCluskey, was called back to California.

When President Mackey traveled to Fordham in 1956 to complete his Ph.D., Father Tutas became acting-president; he relates that "I was able to bring together the administration, the faculty and the entire student body in one classroom."

While Fr. Tutas acknowledges that the biggest challenge at first was "survival," it was also a very exciting time. "We were a very idealistic group. We were dreamers with a lot of enthusiasm for young people ... and a community of people who wanted to learn together."

Facing Page: *Freitas Hall was named for St. Louis alumnus Henry Freitas, the contractor who built the original campus buildings in 1927.*

Rev. Robert R. Mackey, S.M., S.T.L., Ph.D.
1921-1995

Father Robert Mackey was not simply an outstanding administrator and teacher, but a committed servant who put his belief in social justice into action. During and after serving for over 10 years as president of Chaminade College, Father Mackey was widely respected for his work in ethics, prison reform, and ecumenical understanding.

He chaired the City and County Ethics Commission, the City Charter Commission, and the John Howard Association, aiding ex-prisoners. He also chaired the Corrections Task Force of the Hawai'i Council of Churches, and served as district president of the Legal Aid Society. Father Mackey was deeply involved in ecumenical work with other religious leaders. The head of the Hawaii Methodist Mission called Mackey "the greatest bridge builder the state of Hawai'i has ever produced in closing gaps in religious circles." Yet he shunned the spotlight and served meals to the homeless at the Institute for Human Services. He also provided spiritual and personal counseling to the campus community.

Mackey was a scholar and teacher of philosophy, theology, and religion. The annual Mackey Marianist Lectures were established in his honor. The program brings thinkers and authors from around the world to share insights into contemporary and traditional theological topics.

One of 12 siblings, Father Mackey was born September 12, 1921 in Coldwater, Ohio. He was ordained in Fribourg, Switzerland in 1949 where he was awarded the Licentiate in Sacred Theology. Fr. Mackey died in Honolulu on September 7, 1995, a few days before his 74th birthday.

The Five Founders

Brother Joseph A. Becker
1911-2004

Although Bro. Joseph Becker died in 2004 at the age of 93, his presence will continue to be felt through his many contributions to Chaminade. He created the school motto, *Vita In Verbo* (Life in the Word) and co-wrote the lyrics to the *alma mater* with Bro. Sam Lum. He was also a prolific painter and writer, co-authoring *New Wars: A History of the Marianists in Hawaii 1883-1958*. His student secretary, Mary Lou Torres, submitted the winning name "Silversword" as the school's emblem in a 1962 contest. He, in turn, wrote a poem about its symbolism, *Ho'okupu No Ka Moi*. His poem and painting are on display in the Silversword Café.

Bro. Becker was a professor of English and master teacher of literature, writing and speech from 1955 until he retired in 1979. Bro. Joe was a poet, artist, and an avid bridge and tennis player. His paintings, particularly seascapes and the Madonna & Child, were sold to raise money for the poor in India and the Philippines. After retiring, he served at St Anthony's Parish on Maui, conducting prayer groups and community outreach.

Before arriving in Hawai'i in 1955, Bro. Becker completed his undergraduate education at the University of Dayton in 1934, received an M.A. from Catholic University in 1947, and a Ph.D. from Case-Western Reserve University in 1955 where he became adept at Middle English.

Bro. Joe celebrated 75 years as a Marianist in April 2004 by renewing his vows at a ceremony in Mystical Rose Oratory. He was born on May 10, 1911 in Brooklyn, New York and died in Honolulu on September 24, 2004.

Brother Henry J. Honnert, S.M.
1916-1969

With the appointment of Brother Henry Honnert to the chairmanship of the mathematics department in July 1955, the faculty of the new St. Louis Junior College was complete. Brother Honnert was born June 5, 1916 in Cincinnati. He made his Perpetual Profession of Vows on August 25, 1940. Honnert arrived in Hawai'i in August 1955, from Chaminade High School in Los Angeles where he had taught physics and mathematics, and directed the athletic program. During his previous 19 years as a Marianist he had taught at schools in Puerto Rico, New York, Ohio and California. Bro. Honnert provided the practical zeal so important in the physical expansion of Chaminade College. In addition to his duties as the mathematics instructor, he was responsible for the building of the women's restrooms and lounge, and the biology laboratory tables. Later he headed the Admissions Office and personally recruited students from the Mainland. He held degrees from the University of Dayton and the University of Pittsburgh. Bro. Henry Honnert died suddenly in 1969 at age 53 while jogging in Honolulu.

Brother John McCluskey, S.M.
1912-1998

Brother John McCluskey was the first Dean of Faculty and social studies instructor at St. Louis Junior College. He came to Honolulu in 1953 to serve at St. Louis High School and two years later was tapped to help in the formation of the new two-year college.

Bro. John possessed a gift for initiating and nurturing new ventures. After two years at Chaminade, he left to become Director of Scholastics at St. Mary's University in Moraga, California and head of the Office of Education (1957-62). He was the first principal of Archbishop Riordan High School in San Francisco and then secondary schools supervisor for the San Francisco archdiocese (1962-63). In 1964, he became the founding headmaster of St. Paul's College in Melbourne, as well as the first Marianist to serve in Australia.

Brother John returned to Chaminade in 1970 and continued teaching until his retirement in 1984, returning to California in 1987. Brother John is remembered for his love of learning and encyclopedic knowledge. He organized weekly discussion groups to consider books on intellectual and spiritual issues and was an avid reader and storyteller. He received his B.A. from the University of Dayton, an M.A. from Western Reserve University and continued his graduate studies at UC-Berkeley and Oxford.

Brother McCluskey, who was born in Nebraska in 1912, was a Marianist for 62 years. He died February 16, 1998 in Cupertino, California at age 87.

Father Stephen Tutas, S.M.
1926-

Father Stephen Tutas remains an active voice in the Marianist community and a link to the founding of Chaminade University. Today, after many years on the Mainland, he has returned to Hawai'i and serves at St. Anthony's Parish on Maui. Father Tutas was also acting president and dean of St. Louis Junior College from 1956 to 1957, while Father Robert Mackey completed his Ph.D. at Fordham University.

Before being appointed to the fledgling St. Louis Junior College as professor of religion and modern languages, Father Tutas taught at St. Louis High School from 1947, with the exception of studies abroad. He and Bro. Joseph Becker created the first library for the school by selecting college level books from St. Louis High School, refurbishing them and transporting them to Henry Hall. While in Hawai'i Fr. Tutas also served as Director of the Marianist Community.

In 1962, Fr. Tutas was assigned to the Marianist Seminary in Fribourg, Switzerland. He returned to the U.S. in 1969 to serve as Assistant for Religious Life for the Pacific Province, before being elected Superior General of the Society of Mary—a position he held for 10 years. In 1989 he was awarded the *Pro Ecclesia et Pontifice* medal for outstanding service to the Church. This Papal award recognized the significant strides Father Tutas made in promoting an understanding of religious life and collaboration among religious congregations and bishops in the U.S. and internationally.

Father Stephen Tutas celebrated his 60th year as a Marianist priest in 2004 with ceremonies at Mystical Rose Oratory and in Dayton, Ohio.

and The Founding Students ...

Thirty male students entered St. Louis Junior College in September 1955. Within two years the school had become a four-year co-educational institution and changed its name to Chaminade College. In 1959, three students from the original class graduated with baccalaureate degrees in a ceremony held on the lanai of the administration building, Freitas Hall. All three went on to successful careers in Hawai'i. Long-time benefactor, and now Emeritus member of the Board of Regents, Edward K.O. Eu was the first commencement speaker.

The original entering students were Orlando Almarza, Denis Baptiste, Robert Bonifacio, Gerald Ching, Lester Forrest, Herbert Foster, Raybern Freitas, Patrick Hickey, Ronald Iida, Edward Inatsuka, George Kitkowski, Alvin Kort, William Lee, Edwin Liu, Robert Lum, Bernard Lum Hoy, Abraham Macalutas, Frank Machado, Calvin Mann, Bernard Mendonca, Norman Nakata, Francis Pang, Henry Reeves, Bibiano Reyes, Herman Toma, Steven Vidinha, Harold Wong, Wendell Wong, Toshiyasu Yokoyama and Donald Young.

Above: *L-R: Leonard Rosa, Steve Vidinha and Bernard Lum Hoy at their 1959 commencement.*

Bernard Lum Hoy '59

Bernard Lum Hoy almost re-enlisted in the Marine Corps in 1955; however, on the day he was to be sworn in, his uncle, Thomas Young, a strong St. Louis supporter, drove him to the new St. Louis Junior College. Bernard took the entrance exam on the spot, was accepted, and four years later became one of the first three graduates to receive a baccalaureate degree from Chaminade College. While in college, he designed the Chaminade Seal.

Bernard was a liberal arts major and art student. He was chosen by the faculty to create a symbol using a hand holding a flaming sword. The seal was used on their graduation rings and diplomas as well as T-shirts he made for fellow students. He recalls his art teacher: "Brother Nicholas Waldeck was my tutor. He was a great artist."

Born in Hana, Maui, Bernard attended Hana High and then St. Anthony's in Wailuku. After graduation from Chaminade in 1959, he was hired as a police recruit. During his 35 years with HPD he rose from foot patrolman to detective and later assisted programmers in computerizing criminal records. In 1971 he joined the Department's Personnel Division. During his career he added an AA degree in Police Science from Kapi'olani Community College to his bachelor's from Chaminade. Bernard retired in 1985.

Bernard's wife Lolita (class of '61) graduated from Kapa'a High School on Kaua'i in 1957. Accepted at UH, she opted for the newly named Chaminade College because of its small classes. Lolita was in Chaminade's first 4-year coed class.

Above: *Lum Hoy's Chaminade seal.*

Leonard G. Rosa '59

Leonard Rosa was an educator for 30 years before his retirement in 1988. He served as head of the English department at St. Louis High School for 20 years and also served as principal of St. Michael's School in Waialua for three years. At his retirement he was an English instructor at Punahou School. Leon Mederios, a long-time colleague in the St. Louis English Department, notes that "Leonard was a very complicated person—brilliant, talented, interesting, a man of many levels." Leonard was born in Honolulu and died in 1993 at the age of 58. He and his wife Diane (also an English teacher) lived in Kailua and had a daughter and four sons.

Leonard was a staunch supporter of Hawai'i Literacy and an active member of the Portuguese Genealogical Society. After retiring, he researched his family roots and was inspired by the oral history of his grandparents. He compiled several volumes of material for his family and the Portuguese Genealogical Society. Leonard's other avocation was art, and he often presented friends with his line drawings, especially at Christmastime.

Above: *Rosa's Maria Daruma card.*

Steven E. Vidinha '59

Steven Vidinha recalls Brother John McCluskey's recruiting visit to Kaua'i which convinced the recent high school graduate to attend the new St. Louis Junior College. He also remembers "living in the dorms—former housing for nurses during WWII located on the site of Mystical Rose Oratory—with eight other students and Brother Henry Honnert." Steven was the first student body president and graduated with a B.S. in Education. His first job was as a teacher at Olomana High School in the State Juvenile Correctional Facility in Kailua. The following year he joined the Honolulu Police Department and in 1968 was awarded a U.S. Department of Justice Fellowship—one of eight awarded nationwide—to do a year of graduate work at the School of Criminology, University of California-Berkeley.

Upon his return to Hawai'i, Steve was offered a Deputy Directorship by the Governor John Burns in the newly created State Law Enforcement Planning Agency. whose purpose was to administer federal funds to criminal justice agencies in Hawai'i to curb crime and prevent delinquency.

Steve later headed the Statistical Analysis Center for the State Judiciary. He retired in 1991 with nearly 34 years of combined City/State service. Steven notes of his years at Chaminade, "We lacked some of the resources ... that many established universities had ... We gave up a lot to get Chaminade going ... and we didn't mind making sacrifices because it only made Hawai'i and education in Hawai'i stronger."

Three Artistic Brothers

While many Brothers have been good artists, three have stood out over the past half-century—Bro. Joe Becker, Bro. James Roberts, and Bro. Nicholas Waldeck.

Bro. Joe was one of the founders in 1955. An exceptional English teacher and writer, in his later years he became an excellent artist. Brother Nicholas was the precise reverse: An artist who later took an interest in writing, one finger at a time on an old manual typewriter, whose measured clack ... clack ... clack, it is said, drove the other Brothers crazy!

Brother James, now in his 74th year and still active as an artist, left Honolulu in the summer of 2005 for re-assignment in California, where he is to design a Marianist health center for the Brothers in Cupertino.

Above: *Bro. Waldeck's 1938 painting of Punaluʻu on the Windward coast. The Brothers then had a retreat there called* Haleʻaha *(meeting house).*

Brother Waldeck's Fresco

Thousands of students passed the floor-to-ceiling fresco on the lanai wall fronting Sullivan Library in Henry Hall, never knowing the story of determination that created it. Bro. Nicholas Waldeck, who was born in Baltimore in 1895, arrived in Hawaiʻi in 1918, and was reknowned for his religious paintings, Hawaiian landscapes and oil portraits of St. Louis principals.

Bro. Waldeck's contributions to the St Louis-Chaminade campus stretch back to the opening of St. Louis College at the Kaimuki campus in 1928. Respected for his artistic abilities, he became the landscape architect, selecting and planting the first flowers, trees, and shrubs with an eye to harmony and contrast.

When Bro. Waldeck approached Fr. Robert Mackey, then President of Chaminade, about teaching art at the college, he was informed he needed a master's degree to teach on the college level. And so, at the age of 61, he embarked on graduate studies at the University of Hawaiʻi.

Working under renowned artist Jean Charlot, Waldeck began the 12 by 15 foot fresco called "The Lay Apostolate." He based it on the parable of the Good Samaritan, used a Hawaiian motif, and was challenged by the difficult medium. Frescos are created by the application of wet plaster—made of lime, silica and marble—to an existing wall and must remain wet while being painted.

Waldeck applied enough plaster to do a day's work, outlined the detail and then painted on the wet plaster. The fresco was begun in December 1958 and completed in January 1959.

Due to its deteriorating condition, the 45-year-old mural was removed in May 2005. However, high quality photography and digital enhancement techniques were used to create a large framed print with accompanying explanatory text which now hangs in the Sullivan Library.

Brother Waldeck died in Honolulu in 1979 at 84.

Facing Page: *Brother Nicholas Waldeck's fresco.*

Brother Roberts' Mystical Rose Oratory

Designed by Brother James Roberts and erected in 1966, the Mystical Rose Oratory is one of the most visually stunning houses of worship in the Islands. A spectacular profile of Diamond Head fills the viewplane to the right while an intimate tropical garden is on the left. With superb acoustics, the Oratory is often used for both Chaminade and community-wide musical events, including the Hawai'i Vocal Arts Ensemble.

Bro. Roberts' unique design features 13 columns representing Christ and His 12 disciples—despite the fact that the architect strongly urged a change to an even number. Brother Jim also directed the renovation of Mystical Rose in 2000 which included reflooring, new seating, replacement of the windowed walls with tinted glass, and the addition of central air-conditioning. Bro. Jim traveled to Italy, as well, to choose a new stone altar and lectern for the sanctuary.

Arriving in Hawai'i in 1962, Bro. Jim began the art department at Chaminade and for the first few years was its only instructor. "I started with just your basic drawing class," he recalls. A prolific artist himself, Bro. Jim has worked in ink, watercolor, and pencil and has experimented with styles including abstract, pointillism, realism, portrait, landscape and still life.

In addition to painting he has sculpted and worked with serigraph. Today his favorite medium is oil on canvas and his style has evolved into a kind of impressionism. "I like to create something that is an illusion close up, where the subject takes form as you move farther away from the piece."

Bro. Roberts was born in 1931 in Los Angeles and took his Perpetual vows as a Marianist in 1955. In Summer 2005, he was reassigned to service in California and leaves a rich artistic legacy at Chaminade University.

Facing page: *Brother Roberts' Mystical Rose Oratory.*

Above: *Brother Roberts at work.*

Below: *Bro. Roberts' "Water Lilies."*

27

Brother Becker's Paintings

Bro. Joseph Becker was, in the words of co-founder Fr. Steven Tutas, "a consummate teacher." Bro. Joe taught literature and writing and led the English department for 25 years, from 1955 until his retirement in 1980. But his avocation was painting.

He traced his love of art to his grandfather who worked as a tailor, but had studied art at Cooper Union and continued it as a hobby. As a child, Bro. Joe watched and learned. While teaching at Chaminade, and continuing into his retirement, Bro. Joe recalled, 'I had been doing miniature painting and had been hanging them up in my room but I was running out of walls! So when the Marianist community wanted to raise money to send to the poor in India, I offered my paintings, and it just grew from there." He continued to sell paintings on campus and at the Pauline Book and Media Center in Honolulu with all proceeds going to charity—particularly to the poor in India and the Philippines.

Often his love of poetry and art intersected. His painting of the silversword (1984) hangs in the Silversword Café accompanied by the poem he wrote after the 'ahinahina (Hawaiian for "very gray") was adopted as the school emblem in 1960. The plant is native to Hawai'i and, in particular, the cinder deserts of Haleakala on Maui.

Right: *Brother Joe Becker's painting of Chaminade's silversword.*

Campus Fountains & Statuary

The Chaminade campus features numerous gardens with fountains and religious statuary. These include Father Chaminade (lower left); Mary and Child by Yukio Ozaki (below); Jesus (lower right); Mary (above); and Our Lady of the Pillar (upper right).

Drama on the Hill

William Croarkin

Under original director William Croarkin, the drama program at Chaminade found its first permanent home in 1967 in the former chapel in Henry Hall. The sanctuary was converted into a raised stage, and the rows of church pews were removed, as the 200-seat facility soon became known as the "Little Theater." It replaced such earlier homes as the auditorium at Ali'iolani Elementary School.

Croarkin was the rock on which the drama program at Chaminade was built. Arriving in 1965 as an Instructor in English and Drama, he brought an energy and enthusiasm that reached well beyond the school and into the community. He initiated an annual state-wide Shakespeare Festival, bringing together more than 200 students from public and private schools. It was marked by day-long acting competitions, and Elizabethan dress, games and food.

Croarkin frequently double-cast productions to give as many students as possible an opportunity to appear. In one production the cast outnumbered the audience but Croarkin insisted, "Drama is primarily for the students not critics; when we stage a play, I hope the production will bring the students into contact with good literature."

Himself an actor, Croarkin appeared during the early 1970s in numerous roles on the television series *Hawaii 5-0* and played Brother Joseph Dutton in the film *Damien*. He also brought prominent actors to Chaminade to receive the St.

Above: *Fr. Mackey, international star Julie Andrews and Fr. Schuyler at the presentation of the first St. Genesis Award to Andrews.*

Genesis Award, the first awarded to Julie Andrews. Other guest speakers included Marcel Marceau, Beatrice Lillie, Loretta Young, Lucille Ball and Sir Michael Redgrave.

His first production, *Trojan Women*, presented a look at the ravages of war, a theme which resonated in 1967 as the war in Vietnam was escalating. The cast of 32 featured students Ed Williams, Laura Bonomo, Linda Donahue, and Leslie Kula with musical advisor Bro. Victor Bourdon.

In his review of *A Man for All Seasons*, Dave Donnelly, *Honolulu Star-Bulletin* columnist (and actor) remarked, "(Chaminade is) reaching for the meat of dramatic literature. Such an appetite is not to be discouraged."

Croarkin continued to direct productions and teach at Chaminade until his retirement. He died in Rome in 1978.

Above: To be Young, Gifted and Black *was one of Linda Ryan's first and most successful productions.*

Linda Ryan

He was succeeded by British-born actress and director Linda Ryan, who arrived at Chaminade as chair of the Fine Arts Department in 1980. She was in the midst of a successful local stage and television career which featured regular guest roles on *Hawaii 5-0*, *Magnum P.I.* and *Jake and the Fatman*. Over her decade at Chaminade she directed a number of excellent productions. Ryan left to run Honolulu's alcohol-free First Night, and was succeeded by local actor Tracy Anderson.

After a 15-year hiatus, Chaminade reinitiated a campus-based drama program in 2002. Father Robert Bouffier, S.M. joined the faculty as a half-time visiting associate professor and produced *A Midsummer Night's Dream* staged with a Hawaiian setting. Fr. Bouffier, who had taught drama at the University of Dayton and has directed more than 50 productions, spends one semester a year at Chaminade and the other at the Marianist Scholasticate in Bangalore, India.

In 2003 Brother Gary Morris joined the faculty as a full-time associate drama professor in residence. He has over 24 years of teaching experience in theater, English and speech and has directed more than 80 productions. His latest production was *Godspell*, performed at Mamiya Theater.

Smaller productions are staged in Chaminade's Black Box Theatre.

A Midsummer Night's Dream

Above and Below: *Godspell 2005*

The Sound of Music

West Side Story

You're a Good Man, Charlie Brown

Brother Gary Morris

Father Robert Bouffier

Right: *In 1983 Ryan staged the first Chaminade production of* Guys and Dolls, *a musical she had starred in more than once herself.*

God's Eye View of the Campus

Hardly had the steamshovels, dump trucks and cement mixers rumbled off Kalaepohaku after moving out craggy boulders and creating the first buildings of St. Louis College, than biplanes began chugging overhead with a photographer hanging out of the rear seat. Kalaepohaku has been a magnet for aerial photographers ever since.

Aerial images of the campus show in great detail the growth of both Saint Louis and Chaminade across some three-quarters of a century. What is deceptive—especially to anyone who has hiked up and down it—is that they do not show the steepness of the hill!

Above: *Circa 1929-30. At upper left, Newel (then the Science Building), the fifth major structure, is already in place.*

Below: *Circa 1962, just prior to the construction of Hale Hoaloha.*

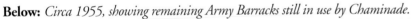

Below: *Circa 1955, showing remaining Army Barracks still in use by Chaminade.*

Above: *As the campus appeared from the air in 2004. The major additions since the 1965 aerial are Mystical Rose (1966), two dorms—Hale Lokelani (1967) and Hale Pohaku (1975) and the Regency Park condos to left of driveway (1979).*

More recently, four modular buildings have been assembled on the upper campus. These have been roofed and faced in the same Spanish Mission style as Bertram, Freitas and Henry Halls. A great deal of interior renovation has also been done.

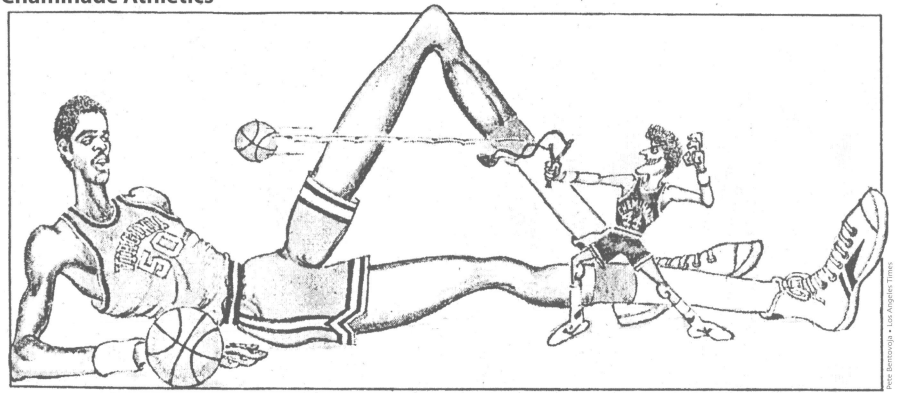

Pete Bentovoja • Los Angeles Times

Chaminade Did It With a Slingshot

Despite hundreds of intercollegiate and intra-mural Chaminade sports teams over half a century, one single victory will likely always stand out: the amazing 77-72 win over No. 1-ranked Virginia led by the three-time College basktball Player of the Year, 7-foot-4 Ralph Sampson.

It was two days before Christmas 1982 in Honolulu. Visiting Virginia had scheduled the game as an easy warm-up win and was stunned—as was the sports world—when Chaminade coach Merv Lopes turned his team loose against the mighty Cavaliers, who were just a couple of weeks past beating Georgetown and Patrick Ewing in what had been billed as "The Game of the Decade." Now, in Honolulu's Blaisdell Arena, they were on

the losing end of what has been known ever since as "The Greatest Upset in the History of College Basketball."

Chaminade's starting five was Tim Dunham, Richard Haenisch, Tony Randolph, Mark Rodrigues and Mark Wells. Randolph and Sampson had played for arch-rival high schools in their native Virginia, and on this night, Randolph outscored the big man 19-12. The one play that marked the game was Rodrigues' alley-oop to the 6' 2" Dunham, who slam-dunked over Sampson.

Still astonished many years later, Coach Lopes said, "I still can't explain it. I guess it was meant to be."

Chaminade is an NCAA Division II program and a member of the Pacific West Conference. Men's sports include basketball, water polo, tennis and cross-country, while women field teams in volleyball, softball, tennis and cross-country. Each November, Chaminade hosts the nationally televised Maui Invitational Basketball Tournament. This popular tourney attracts top collegiate teams competing for the pre-season title and is Maui's largest annual event revenue source. The 22nd tournament in November 2005 will include Arizona, Arkansas, Connecticut, Gonzaga, Kansas, Maryland and Michigan State, rounding out a field consisting of six former national champions.

Above: *Celebrating victory over Virginia.*

CHAMINADE ATHLETIC DIRECTORS

1975 - 88	Mike Vasconcellos
1988- 90	Lucius Spence (Acting)
1990 -91	T. Michael Hogan (Acting)
1991- 94	Charles English
1994 - 97	Donald Doucette
1997- 2000	Allan Walker
2000-05	Aaron Griess
2005-	Matt Mahar

Off-Campus & Way Off-Campus

Chaminade was a very early adopter of off-campus learning and has been offering evening and weekend classes since 1967. This Accelerated Undergraduate Program is primarily for military students, and some 2,000 are enrolled each year on more than 10 sites on military bases and at parishes around the Island. The program is newly expanded to Kapolei.

Many courses may be taken on-line—a program Chaminade pioneered in 1995—and members of the military often continue their education when deployed overseas.

CHAPTER IV

The Many Faces of Chaminade

For half a century Chaminade has been many things—buildings, classes, intellectual and spiritual passion, friendships and learning—but most of all Chaminade has been people. The original five dedicated Marianist founders, and their 30 eager young freshmen in 1955, have grown exponentially over the years. An unending march of on-campus—and now, on-line—students, faculty, staff, administrators, regents and trustees have kept the spirit of Chaminade—both the man and the institution—intact and growing.

Like the hill on which it is ensconced, Chaminade's progress has been challenging at times, but the people who have been so much a part of the experience have kept the school advancing, improving, and expanding. Herewith some of the representative faces of Chaminade over the decades.

Above: *Graduation Day 1985. From left: Lisa Hornberger, Joan Nacino, Marcy Salazar, Rose Pagdilao.*

Facing Page and Above: *Secluded grottos for studying, reflecting, and laughing with friends have been created all around campus.*

Above: *Father David Schuyler (far right) greets new faculty in September 1964. From left to right, front row: Dr. Theymouraz de Tsouloukidze, Helen Sakai, Nora Chee, Lee Brenneisen, Dr. Magdelen Eichert, Thomas Guglielmo, Fr. John Rielly, S.M. Back row: F. Brad Wilson, Fr. Francis Chun, S.M.*

Chaminade Presidents

Rev. Robert R. Mackey, S.M., S.T.L., Ph.D.
President: 1955 – 1966

Rev. Robert Mackey arrived in Hawai'i in 1954 to serve as a religion instructor at St. Louis School College and one year later became the founding president of St. Louis Junior College. At the age of 34, he was the nation's youngest college president.

During Father Mackey's 11-year presidential tenure, Chaminade evolved from an all-male two-year college of 31 students to a coeducational, four-year college enrolling over 650 students. In 1956, he took a leave of absence to earn a doctorate in moral philosophy from New York's Fordham University, then returned to Hawai'i in 1957 to teach and continue his leadership of the new 4-year liberal arts college. He realized the importance of reaching out to the community and in 1956, initiated a Chaminade-sponsored, statewide speech contest. That tradition survives 50 years later as the Mackey Speech Competition, open to Chaminade undergraduates.

After his term as president, Father Mackey served as Provincial Assistant for Religious Life for the Province of the Pacific in Santa Cruz, California. One year later, in 1968, he returned to Hawai'i to become Chancellor of the St. Louis-Chaminade Education Center until 1973. Father Mackey then assumed the duties of Director of Special Ministries and contributed to the growth of the school's campus ministry and spiritual outreach. His door was always open to students and faculty for advice and counsel.

His death in Honolulu in 1995 at age 73 left a void in the Chaminade community, but also a rich legacy based on his generous spirit.

Rev. William F. Ferree, S.M. Ph.D.
President: 1966 – 1968

Rev. William F. Ferree brought to his position as Chaminade's second president a broad range of leadership experience. Before arriving here, he held two other college presidencies—at Marianist College (now University of Dayton East Campus) and Rector of Catholic University of Puerto Rico. He then served in Rome as General Assistant for the Offices of Education and Apostolic Action of the Society of Mary. This took him to over 30 countries.

It was Father Ferree's vision that created the St. Louis-Chaminade Education Center, a collaborative arrangement which preceded the present independent status of each school. He advocated more student involvement in university planning by granting a student government member voting privileges on the university's executive council. Fr. Ferree continued as chaplain general of Pax Romana, an international federation of Catholic students. After leaving Chaminade Father Ferree became Provincial of the Cincinnati Province.

A dynamic leader and prolific writer on social issues, Father Ferree is still widely regarded as a scholar on social justice and ethical reform. His 1947 *Introduction to Social Justice* was republished in 1997, and is still a classic text for teachers of social justice, offering practical guidelines for changing basic economic and social institutions. In 1984 he co-founded the Center for Social and Economic Justice, a think tank in Arlington, Virginia.

Born in Dayton, Ohio in 1905, Father Ferree was ordained in 1937, and received his M.A. and Ph.D. degrees in philosophy at Catholic University of America. He died in 1985 at the age of 80.

Bro. Robert C. Maguire, S.M., Ph.D.
President: 1968 – 1974

Bro. Robert Maguire was selected the third president of Chaminade College in 1969, and was the first Marianist Brother to hold the position. He arrived in Hawai'i in September 1967 to become vice-president for academic affairs and became acting president in 1968 upon the resignation of Fr. Ferree. He was formally appointed president in September 1969. Bro. Maguire came to the presidency at a time when student unrest was sweeping the country in response to the civil rights movement and frustration over the Vietnam War. However, Chaminade continued to grow and in 1972 Tredtin Hall—on the site of the former Army recreation hall—was completed. The combination bookstore-dining hall was shared by St Louis High School and Chaminade College.

Before arriving in Hawai'i, Bro. Maguire had spent 16 years at Marianist high schools in San Francisco and Los Angeles and was particularly involved in coaching sports and debate and headed the National Forensic League, earning its highest award.

Prior to coming to Chaminade, Bro Maguire had served at Chaminade Prep in Los Angeles. During that time he completed his Ph.D. in Speech. He also received a master's degree in History in 1949.

Bro. Maguire was born in 1919 in San Francisco and in 1937 entered the Society of Mary. He graduated from the University of Dayton in 1940 and, like Brothers before him, held assignments in Ohio, Puerto Rico and California.

Rev. Charles J. Lees, S.M., Ph.D.
President: 1975 – 1977

Father Charles Lees became the fourth president of Chaminade in March 1975, seeing the school make the transition from college to university. Before coming to Chaminade, Fr. Lees served as an English professor and Provost at the University of Dayton from 1965-1974. As vice-president for administration and planning there, he oversaw the computerization of registration and was credited with reforming tenure and promotion policies for the faculty and introducing several graduate programs. Under his leadership, in 1977 Chaminade College added a graduate degree to its program and achieved the status of university.

Father Lees, then 55, succeeded acting-president Bro. Oliver Aiu, who had led the school since Bro. Robert Maguire's resignation in July 1974. Father Lees brought nearly 30 years of experience in elementary school, secondary school and college teaching and administration. He served Chaminade for two years before going into parish ministry in Hawai'i until 1986. He was known as a master retreat director and an outstanding English teacher.

Born in South Fork, Pennsylvania in 1919, Fr. Lees received his undergraduate degree from the University of Dayton in 1942, his master's from the University of Pittsburgh in 1952, and a Ph.D. in English from Ohio State University in 1961. When Father Lees died in Dayton, Ohio on October 16, 1996 at the age of 76, he had been a member of the Society of Mary for 59 years.

Rev. David H. Schuyler, S.M., J.C.D., S.T.L.
President: 1977 – 1981

Rev. David Schuyler, Chaminade University's fifth president, was the first appointed after the transition to a university. He has had many roles during the past 41 years and today is a member of the Board of Regents.

In 1980, as Chaminade celebrated its 25th anniversary, Fr. Schuyler reflected on the institution in the year 2005, predicting it would not only survive, but evolve as long as the university remained "faithful to the values and spirit of its foundation."

During his presidency, small colleges across the country were experiencing enrollment and financial difficulties. However, when Fr. Schuyler left office, enrollment had stabilized and the budget had been balanced. Fr. Schuyler first came to Chaminade in 1964 as executive vice-president and academic dean and served until 1966. He left to become assistant chancellor, and later chancellor, of the Honolulu Diocese, then returned to the campus in 1970 as theology instructor and Dean of Faculty. He served as vice-president from 1974 until becoming president in 1977. Fr. Schuyler also served as Assistant for Religious Life for the Marianist Province of the Pacific.

Born in Pomona, California, Father Schuyler entered the Society of Mary after graduating from St. Joseph High School in Alameda and receiving his undergraduate degree at St. Mary's College. He studied at the University of Fribourg in Switzerland and received his doctorate in canon law from the Lateran University of Rome. Today he serves on the Board of Directors of Chaminade College Preparatory in West Hills, California.

Rev. Raymond A. Roesch, S.M., Ph.D.
President: 1982 – 1989

Rev. Raymond Roesch came out of retirement at age 67 to become Chaminade's sixth president. From 1959 to 1979, Fr. Roesch had served as president of the University of Dayton, where enrollment increased to just under 10,000, endowments by 700% to become one of the ten largest Catholic universities in the U.S. In 1979 the University of Dayton named its library in Fr. Roesch's honor.

Fr. Roesch explained his decision to serve Chaminade by remarking that he had "done and seen a lot. Why not the land of Aloha?" Chaminade, then just over 25 years old and the only Marianist university in Hawai'i, benefited from Fr. Roesch's wealth of experience. At the end of his tenure, he had achieved his stated goal of bringing financial stability to the school.

Improvements on campus included major renovation of residence halls, Hale Pohaku and Lokelani, as well as upgrading and repairs to university facilities. Water polo and women's volleyball were added, and a Master of Science in Criminal Justice Administration was established. Fr. Roesch also imparted his philosophy of the role of Catholic schools: "They are not a place where one should be spoon-fed all the answers. They are places to ask questions and grow."

Born in Pennsylvania on September 16, 1914. Fr. Roesch received his bachelor's from the University of Dayton, a master's from Catholic University of America, and a doctorate from Fordham University. He had a distinguished career as a psychologist, educator and administrator. He died in Dayton in July 1991 at the age of 76.

Kent M. Keith, J.D., M.A.
President: 1990 – 1995

On January 28,1990 Bishop Joseph Ferrario of the Roman Catholic Diocese of Honolulu inaugurated Kent Keith, 41, as Chaminade University's first Protestant president and first layman to hold that position.

During Keith's term, evening and graduate enrollment rose to an all-time high, despite a declining day enrollment, due, in part, to demographics in the 18 to 24-year-old age group. Salaries were also raised substantially and staffing reduced by 25%. A successful capital campaign lead to renovations on the campus. Master's degrees in teaching and public administration were added.

Keith was director of the State Department of Planning and Economic Development, after practicing law from 1977 to 1979. Prior to coming to Chaminade, he served as an executive with Oceanic Properties, Inc., a land development subsidiary of Castle and Cooke from 1979 to 1986.

Keith graduated from Roosevelt High School, earned a B.A. in Government from Harvard University, and an M.A. in Philosophy and Politics from Oxford University where he was a Rhodes scholar. He received his law degree from the University of Hawai'i.

After leaving Chaminade, Keith went on to receive an Ed.D. from the University of Southern California. In 2002 he published *The Paradoxical Commandments*. He is president of Carlson Keith Corporation, a company dedicated to motivational and leadership enterprises. He and his wife have three children and live in Honolulu.

Mary Civille "Sue" Wessselkamper, D.S.W.
President: 1995 – present

The Board of Regents unanimously approved the selection of Dr. Sue Wesselkamper in July 1995 as the eighth president of Chaminade. She became the first woman to head a four-year university in Hawaii. Under her leadership, Chaminade has experienced unprecedented growth in enrollment and capital improvements and attained unconditional reaccreditation.

Facing a deficit and deteriorating physical facilities in 1995, Wesselkamper obtained a generous gift from the Marianist Congregation, which resolved the school's operating debt and helped to make possible the school's successful rebound. Enrollment has increased some 65% from about 600 day students to over 1000. Faculty increased at about the same rate to the present 77, with a staff of over 140.

Dr. Wesselkamper holds undergraduate degrees in history and government, and a master's degree in social work, from the University of Michigan. She also holds a doctorate in social work from the Graduate Center, City University of New York. Before she began her academic career, she was a community outreach worker, medical social worker and social services director. From 1987 until her appointment at Chaminade, she served as dean of arts and sciences and associate professor of social work in the College of New Rochelle, New York.

Wesselkamper enjoys hiking and reading. She and her husband Tom, who is a visiting professor of computer information systems at Chaminade, are the parents of two grown children.

Faces Over the Years

Adams, Glennie
Athletics

Aiu, Bro. Oliver
Administration

Ammon, Sister
Personnel

Aukai, Lori
Facilities

Barber, Paul
Staff

Benitez-Hodge, Grissel
Administration

Bigelow, Marilyn
Library

Agor, Cathy
Campus Ministry

Alameida, Corrine
Staff

Anderson, David
Religion

Baier, Maggie
AUP

Bard, Imre
History

Bevins, Marilyn
Staff

Bogart, Louise
Education

Ahakuelo, Kapika
Staff

Alau, Maile
Staff

Asselin, Pierre
History

Baker, Marlene
Staff

Becker, Bro. Joseph
English

Beyer, Bro. Anthony
History

Bolin, Rev. John
Administration

Ai, Vinette
Staff

Allen, Kevin
Library

Au, Marianne
Education

Bailey, Frank
History

Becker, Ron
Criminal Justice

Bieberly, Cliff
Communication

Bommer, Bro. Jerry
Administration

44

Bordner, Rick
Anthropology

Bretschneider, Yveline
French

Callahan, Caryn
Business

Cervantes, Joyce
Staff

Chang, Bro. Leonard
Campus Ministry

Christiana, Bro. Jim
Sociology

Coleman, Valerie
Library

Borns, Charlie
Staff

Bugado, Dominic
Staff

Carey, Dick
History

Cha, Nancy
Student Support Service

Charron, Alita
Staff

Chun-Hoon, Harry
Biology

Cooke, David
Physics

Bouey, Joy
Administration

Bulosan, Marcia
Staff

Carney, Tim
Music

Chaminade, Fr. W. Joseph
Namesake

Chatfield, Sr. Joan
Religion

Claspell, Emily
Psychology

Cordova, Gary
Administration

Bouffier, Fr Robert
Drama

Calbero, Evangeline
Staff

Castle, Lilia
History

Chandler, Robert
English

Chee, Nora
Biology

Coleman, David
Religion

Croarkin, William
Drama

Damm, Bro. Frank
Administration

Downey, Steve
Staff

Facette, Bro. Jim
Administration

Ferree, Fr. William
Administration

Friedman, Peggy
Business

Garcia, Amelia
Staff

Goldsborough, Dorothy
Criminal Justice

DeCosta, Michelle
Staff

Dunsky, Bro. Elmer
Education

Fagin, Jim
Criminal Justice

Flynn, Joan
Library

Frierson, Eleanor
French

Garlach, Stacia
Communication

Gomes, Henry
Biology

Degorio, Bro. Jose
Staff

Eden, Fr. Tim
Education

Fassiotto, Mike
Administration

Francis, Allison
English

Fryxell, Dale
Psychology

Gerber, Bro. Herman
Administration

Gomes, Fr. Herman
Campus Ministry

Derby, Sr. Roberta Julie
English/Criminal Justice

Engelcke, Fr. John
Religion

Ferguson, William
Business

Fredricks, Dorothy
History

Fuchigami, Brian
English

Goff, Lee
Forensic Science

Gonzales, Greg
Facilities

Grabowsky, Gail
Environmental Science

Hansen, Neil
Business

Harvey, Kim
Anthropology

Hernandez, Jorge
Staff

Honda, Glenn
Education

Hubbard, Marian
Library

Ituralde, Venus
Residential Life

Griess, Aaron
Athletics

Harms, Joan
Staff

Hays-Thomas, Helen
Administration

Hironaka, Sunao
Art

Honnert, Bro. Henry
Mathematics

Hutter, Dean
Business

Iwamoto, Linda
English

Haines, Ruth
Mathematics

Harp, Karen
Staff

Heinle, Bro.Tom
Campus Ministry

Hiu, Dawes
Chemistry

Hoppe, Bro. Robert
Administration

Ishihara, Jamei
Staff

Iwamoto, Ronald
Biology

Haisen, Mike
Facilities

Hartung, Martha
Education

Hertweck, Fr. Bob
Marianist Community

Hogan, Fr. Thomas
Religion

Houghton, Alison
Student Support Services

Ito, Esther
Staff

James, Jon
English

Jerome, Allison
Student Support Services

Kauhane, Fred
Security

Kishi, Ann
Staff

Kop, Melba
Communication

Kraughto, Keith
Alumni Relations

Lake, John
Hawaiian Studies

Lee, Nani
Staff

Kakazu, Kerry
CIS

Keith, Kent
Administration

Klauser, Jack
Business

Kopf, Don
Counseling

Kuo, Peter
Sociology

Lau, Collin
Criminal Justice

Lee, Rose
Staff

Kaneakua, Luka
Facilities

Kido, Richard
Business

Kodama, Be-Jay
Alumni Relations

Kort, Blanche
Staff

Kuriyama, Carolyn
Communication

Lawes ,Brock
Business

Lee, Skip
AUP

Karbens, Jack
Business

Kirchner, Regina
Education

Koki, Gail
Staff

Kraus, James
English

Kurosawa, Janine
Staff

Lee, Lorrie
Staff

Lee-Robinson, Patti
Biology

Lees, Fr. Charles
Administration

Lopes, Merv
Athletics

Mackey, Fr. Robert
Administration

Man, Bryan
Sociology

Martin, Jan
Staff

McCluskey, Bro. John
History

Mellom, Debbie
Staff

LePage, Sharon
Library

Lowry, Deborah
Interior Design

Maglasang, Andrea
Staff

Marceau, Alan
Staff

Martins, Paolo
CIS

McCully, Joanne
Advising

Miller, Ginger
Staff

Lincoln, Peter
Computer Science

Lum, Albert
English

Maguire, Bro. Robert
Administration

Mark, Greg
Criminal Justice

Maruyama, Bro. Robert
CIS

McGinnis, Dean
Staff

Miller, James
Physics

Loo, Archie
Staff

Lum-Kee, Fr. Charles
Religion

Mahar, Matt
Athletics

Marker, David
Adminstration

Masuchika, Glenn
Library

Meacham, Larry
Political Science

Mistysyn, Linda
Library

Miura, Carol
Student Support Services

Moody, Peggy
Psychology

Moscove, Brenda
Business

Nakama, Priscilla
Staff

Nodel, Julius
Religion

Ortogero, Renee
Staff

Petrie, Loretta
English

Miyakawa, Gay
Administration

Mori, Art
Chemistry

Moses, James
Business

Nakasone, Jon
Educational Technology

O'Connell, Fr. Bill
Marianist Community

Osborne, Larry
Administration

Pfeiffer, Regina
Religion

Mize, Margaret
Education

Morris, Bro. Gary
Drama

Murray, Bill
Business

Natadecha-Sponsel, Poranee
Sociology/Religion

Oide, Nancy
Student Support Services

Ozaki, Yukio
Art

Platte, Sara
Staff

Monahan, Bruce
Business

Morris, John
Staff

Nagasawa, Art
History

Nicole, Ann
Psychology

Ornellas, Trudy
Staff

Pao, Bro. Franklin
Marianist Community

Ploeger, Bro. Bernard
Administration

Rex, Ron
Administration

Roesch, Fr. Raymond
Adminstration

Ryan, Linda
Drama

Schmitz, Bro Dennis
Special Ministries

Schroeder, Scott
Business

Silbereis, Bro.Fred
Mathematics

Smerz, Angela
Staff

Richards, Sarah
Administration

Rosa, Wanda
Staff

Sakamoto, Cassandra
Staff

Schneider, Bro. John
Administration

Schuyler, Fr. David
Administration

Simonelli, Mitzi
Psychology

Smith, Mi-Soo
Mathematics

Roberts, Bro. James
Art

Rubin, Barry
Criminal Justice

Sam, Betty
Staff

Schonleber, Nanette
Education

Shea, Bill
Support Services

Simpson, Kekoa
Records

Smith, Robert
History

Robinson, James
English

Ryan, Kapono
Staff

Sampson, Gwen
Staff

Schroeder, Koreen
English

Shimakawa, Ellen
Biology

Sittler, Eileen
Spanish

Spring, Bro.Tom
Mathematics

Stathakos, Cathy
English

Street, Barbara
Business

Summersgill, Harue
Japanese

Templin, Fr. Kenneth
Campus Ministry

Treverrow, Tracy
Psychology

Tyau, Eleanor
Staff

Urata, Betty
Staff

Steele, Cliff
Athletics

Streeter, Lucille
Personnel

Takayama, Stan
Food Services

Terem, Bulent
Chemistry

Trudeau, Sr. Christina
Education

Tyler, Eiko
Mathematics

Vasconcellos, Mike
Athletics

Steelquist, John
Business

Suda, Jolene
Student Support Services

Takeda, Walter
Art

Torquato, Simone
Staff

Tsushima, Jean
Staff

Uchigakiuchi, Patrick
Psychology

Volkomener, Helen
Administration

Stone, Kay
Campus Ministry

Sullivan, Wilson
Forensic Science

Tanna, Wayne
Business

Touhy, Thalia
Library

Tutas, Fr. Stephen
Administration

Unni, Chitha
Philosophy

Verley, Joy
Staff

52

Von, Marian
Student Support Services

Webster, John
Business

Westbrock, Bro. Edward
History

Won, Johanna
Staff

Yablonsky, Jude
Communication

Yee, Dan
Mathematics

Waldeck, Bro. Nicholas
Art

Weeks, Catherine
Student Support Services

Wheeler, Steve
Staff

Wong, Chock
Mathematics

Yamasaki, Mitch
History

Yoshimura, Donna
AUP

Walker, Al
Athletics

Wesselkamper, Sue
Administration

Wilkinson, Mary
Student Support Services

Wong, Sr. Claudia
Campus Ministry

Yamauchi, Hiroshi
Physics

Young, Kellie
Student Support Services

Washburn, Curtis
Advising

Wesselkamper, Tom
CIS

Won, Greta
Administration

Woolum, Andrea
Student Support Services

Yee, Bette
Staff

53

Some Special Sisters

Sister Christina Trudeau, SND
1930 -

In characteristic fashion, Sr. Christina Trudeau was drawn out of retirement one more time during the Summer of 2005. She led over a dozen men and women from across the nation who converged at Chaminade to participate in the Mission Module sponsored by the Master of Arts in Pastoral Leadership and the Chaminade education department. The 3-week program offered courses designed to help participants develop distance education throughout the Pacific and South East Asia and to enable them to take Montessori training into global mission teaching.

This globetrotting educator has been a Sister of Notre Dame de Namur for over 55 years and was instrumental in bringing the Montessori method to Chaminade and to expanding it in Hawai'i. The Montessori philosophy emphasizes all facets of the child's unfolding personality—spiritual, social, psychological, cognitive, and physical—and the teaching of the whole child.

Sr. Christina first came to Hawai'i in the early 1970s to conduct summer workshops in Montessori teaching methods. Almost 100 people registered for her first course and because the demand was great, Sr. Christina was encouraged to submit a proposal for full-time teacher preparation. This was accepted by the University and the American Montessori Society (AMS), and by 1974 she had recruited the first class of students. Under her leadership, the program continued to grow, and the university's own Lab School was established in 1982. Today the L. Robert Allen Montessori Center is located in Hale Lokelani. Fran DeMattos, director of the pre-school, calls Sr. Christina "the driving force behind Montessori education in Hawai'i."

Sister Roberta Julie Derby, SND
1929 - 1996

Sr. Roberta Julie Derby, S.N.D. joined Chaminade in 1970 as an Assistant Professor of English. Her ability to convey her passion for literature was legendary, as was her ability to relate to students. But Sr. Roberta had another dimension to her life. In 1971 she began serving as volunteer chaplain/counselor with the Honolulu Police Department, and in 1976, began a 20-year, full-time HPD career as Chaplain One. She was also key in establishing the Criminal Justice program at Chaminade.

Honolulu Police Department Museum

In 1989, while retaining her full load at Chaminade, she was appointed to organize the activities of HPD's Human Services Unit, which includes the Chaplain Corps, peer support personnel, and others who perform counseling and guidance services for department members. Sister Roberta was the first female police chaplain in the United States and served until shortly before her death in 1996. She was succeeded by another Chaminade instructor, Fr. Vince O'Neill, who recalls that Sr. Roberta "showed compassion and at the same time, was very much a straight shooter with the officers."

In 1980, Sister Roberta received the HPD Silver Medal of Valor award, when she totally disregarded her own safety and entered an apartment where a distraught man with a gun was holding his son hostage. Sister Roberta removed the child to safety, then negotiated the man's surrender.

Sister Roberta won the heartfelt admiration and respect of those with whom she served, and contributed greatly to the accomplishment of the department's goals. In her honor, the park next to Police Headquarters has been officially named The Sister Roberta Julie Derby, Chaplain One, Park.

Hogan Entrepreneurs

Ed and Lynn Hogan are born entrepeneurs. After catching the flying bug in the Naval Air Corps during World War II, Ed earned his commercial pilot's license and eventually joined Transocean Air Lines, a non-scheduled carrier and the first tourist flight operation to Hawai'i. A trained commercial artist whose credits include working at Disney Studios, Lynn met Ed and they married while both were employees of Transocean. Ed left the cockpit to eventually become director of domestic and Pacific sales, based in New York. When transocean folded in 1959, the Hogans opened their own travel agency called Pleasant Travel Service in Point Pleasant, NJ. Lynn ran the office while Ed developed new business, and organized some of the first groups to travel to Hawai'i.

After years operating what is today the largest travel company serving Hawai'i—Pleasant Hawaiian Holidays—they retired and established the non-profit Hogan Family Foundation to encourage a greater understanding of the entrepreneurial spirit through the creation and operation of educational, civic-minded and humanitarian programs designed to encourage a more productive and contributory society. Since its founding in 1998, the Foundation has invested more than $40 million in its charitable programs.

In keeping with their focus on self-reliance, the Foundation funds programs in Entrepreneurial Studies at Gonzaga University in Spokane, Washington and at Chaminade, where the "Hogan Entrepreneurs" program prepares highly motivated students for entrepreneurial careers in business, government, and non-profit organizations. An interdisciplinary preparation builds capacity to innovate, willingness to take risks, and sensitivity to the social significance of their business activities. Steeped in the tradition of Marianist values, the Hogan program is open to students from all majors. Those chosen take part in a variety of curricular and co-curricular activities during their junior, senior, and/or graduate student years.

In addition to business skills, the program fosters a mind-set that makes integrity and concern for social justice central to all entrepreneurial pursuits.

Above: *The 2003 Hogan Entrepreneurs.*

Above: *Hogan Entrepreneurs. Lynn and Ed Hogan are second row center.*

55

Chapter V

The Second Founding

The idea of a second founding is paradoxical. It involves reaching back and moving forward simultaneously with a goal of ending up significantly ahead of where it begins. Although a second founding is rooted in a recovery of the organization's original mission and identity, it also requires something new. Chaminade experienced a severe institutional crisis during the early and mid-90's. In emerging from this crisis, it returned to its mission in search of clear identity and purpose. To secure its future, the University needed a new vision of how it was to be; one that was sufficiently compelling to justify the effort demanded for personal and institutional transformation and to win the support of its various publics.

The collective will of the Chaminade community to address long standing challenges by re-centering on its mission is reflected in the 1997 strategic plan, "The Second Founding of Chaminade." The vision of that plan drew on the traditional strengths of Chaminade: its inclusive Catholic, Marianist identity and mission where faith, liberal learning, values-centered conversations, community, a concern for the whole person and the development of leadership for service remain core values of the University; where its multicultural campus and community, its location in the Pacific as a gateway to Asia and a faculty culture that highly values teaching and student mentoring, continue to make it distinctive. The vision included improving enrollments, developing faculty and academic offerings, integrating technology into curricula and all aspects of university operations, and financial strategies geared toward balancing budgets, accumulating surpluses, stimulating fund raising, and upgrading campus facilities.

Facing Page: *The chapel at the Marianist Residence,* Hale Malia.

In 1999, the Strategic Plan was revised with an emphasis on "Securing Our Future." As a campus community, Chaminade has moved forward aggressively in implementing this strategic vision. The results of these collective efforts are truly remarkable. In efforts directed toward re-centering on our Catholic, Marianist identity, the Chaminade faculty developed and adopted a statement of *Core Academic Beliefs* designed to be used as underlying curriculum principles. In 1999 faculty also collaborated with faculty from the other two Marianist universities in developing a resource paper on the *Characteristics of Marianist Universities.* Other University activities also reflect a renewed focus on our identity as a Catholic, Marianist University. Campus ministry, in developing its programs, plays a key role in these re-centering efforts. Service learning activities, which exemplify the Marianist ideal of educating students to serve their communities, have significantly expanded. Through guest speakers, visiting Marianists, and shared programming with the Marianist Center's Office of Special Ministries, there are more opportunities for faculty and staff to come together to learn about and reflect on the nature of Marianist educational principles. Orientation programs for new faculty and staff, campus community celebrations and recognition programs are held throughout the year as expressions of our mission statement.

The addition of Marianist brothers and priests to Chaminade's faculty and administration have been a key component of the re-centering on its heritage. Through the initiation of Chaminade's President Kent Keith, informal meetings with the presidents and administrators of the other two Marianist universities (University of Dayton and St. Mary's University San Antonio) began in the early 1990's. These meetings evolved into a formal Association of Marianist Universities in 2004. Key features include an executive director to provide leadership and the annual meeting of administrators, faculty and staff from the three Universities on a theme related to strengthening mission and identity.

The very visible physical changes to campus convey a sense of excitement and are reflective of the significant growth in the academic area. The size of full time faculty has grown by more than 50%. Professors, committed to the deepening of their professional peer culture, have taken advantage of expanded faculty development opportunities. In 2004, the University was successful in recruiting its first Fulbright Scholar in Residence.

Since 2001, the faculty of the academic divisions, with the assistance of Bro. Bernard Ploeger as Executive Vice President and Provost, have reviewed essentially all graduate programs and undergraduate majors. Many of these reviews resulted in significant restructuring of the curricula. The introduction of a Forensic Science major has drawn national interest from both undergraduate students and working professionals. Faculty have also taken leadership in developing and supporting programs to enrich majors by offering students research and professional career opportunities. The McNair Program, now in its tenth year, provides up to 20 students each year the opportunity to engage in research activities under the guidance of faculty members during the summer months.

At the initiation of committed science faculty, each summer 20-25 students participate in funded pre-med and science research internships at leading universities including Johns Hopkins, Baylor, University of Hawai'i, University of Virginia, and Yale.

The Hogan Entrepreneurs Program, open to all majors, provides students with hands on experience to develop leadership and business skills. Students of the Interior Design program offer their design services to non-profit organizations. Education faculty and students have formed partnerships with Palolo Elementary school to assist its students in developing their reading and mathematics competencies. These are but a few examples of the intellectual vitality and seriousness of purpose with which faculty have engaged students in learning, encouraging them to participate in service opportunities and preparing them for successful careers.

To guide the renovatation of existing and construction of new buildings to support its academic and co-curricular programs, Chaminade, in collaboration with its partners Saint Louis School and the Marianist Center of Hawai'i, completed a facilities campus master plan in 1999. The Chaminade Board of Regents took a vital role in raising funds for the realization of this vision. Since 1999 Chaminade has made over $25 million in investments to improve and build new facilities, the funding coming from generous friends of Chaminade as well as corporate and private foundations in Hawai'i and on the Mainland. Many improvements have been made to existing buildings on campus. The School of Business offices in Kieffer Hall were extensively renovated (2000), and four modular buildings have been added to the campus: the Student Support Services and Behavioral Sciences buildings (2001), Education building (2002), and the Harold K.L. Castle Science Center building (2003). In addition, extensive renovations are on-going in Freitas and Henry Halls (2004-2005). Three parking areas have also been added, and all additions have been complemented with extensive landscaping and beautification. The Vi and Paul Loo Student Center in Freitas Hall is scheduled to be dedicated in August 2005. The science labs on the ground floor of Henry Hall are undergoing major renovations. Groundbreaking of the $10 million, 30,000 square foot Library will take place in May of 2006.

There is much to be done as Chaminade moves into the future. Still to be funded are a 60,000 square foot Campus Life Center and new on-campus residence halls to house an additional 300 students, a recreational sports facility and, at the request of many students, a swimming pool.

Beyond facilities, Chaminade faces the challenge to continue to develop its academic programs to deepen its distinctive Catholic, Marianist approach to education and build partnerships with the Church and civic communities in Hawai'i and the Pacific Islands, as it grows to its goal of 1500 day undergraduate students.

(Mostly) Recent Campus Construction

Above: *In the "old days" at Chaminade, every hand was called to service. When the college went co-ed in 1957, a ladies room was called for, so Bro. Henry Honnert, wielded a jackhammer to help construct it.*

Below: *Renovations give useful new life to the classic older buildings on campus.*

Right Column: *Modular buildings are both practical and easy to create. Four have been added within the past few years. The top photo shows a crane lowering one of the modules into place for the Harold K.L. Castle Science Learning Center. Next is the completed building with Spanish Mission touches. Below that, the new Student Support Services Building and at bottom, the modular Education Building.*

Above and Below: *Rocks! An entire hillside of them faced the men responsible for the original St. Louis College campus. They are still there, and each new building site requires huge equipment to move them.*

TOM PATTERSON • PATTERSON GRAPHICS

Right: *The Eiben Fountain "Whimsical Nature" by artist Mark Stasz. It was constructed on campus in 2005 of bronze, stainless steel, and granite and was donated by Jean E. Rolles, M.S.J.B.S. '93.*

Serving Native Hawaiian & Pacific Island Students

Chaminade is one of the most ethnically diverse universities in the country. Approximately 17% of Chaminade's undergraduate student body report that they are of Native Hawaiian descent and another 8% report that they are descendents of other indigenous Pacific peoples.

Kumu Hula John Lake

The University supports a wide range of student clubs based upon and affirming the various ethnic groups which make up the student body. The University has a regular set of pageants and extravaganzas in which the music and dance of student ethnic groups are celebrated and displayed. In January 2003, the University initiated a position of *"Kumu in Residence"* which is filled by John Lake, a distinguished native Hawaiian teacher and kumu hula, who is charged with providing program leadership and direction for Hawaiian studies and cultural activities. In collaboration with the Association of Hawaiian Civic Clubs, Chaminade received an Association of Native Americans grant from the U.S. Department of Health and Human Services that supports the initiation of a leadership training program for students of Hawaiian descent while at the same time strengthening community organizations through their services.

Below: *Chaminade's Samoan Club performing at BYU-Hawai'i in 2003.*

Henry Hall

Above: *Henry Hall's long-time chapel was converted to a theatre once Mystical Rose opened. The space now serves as the first floor of the Sullivan Library.*

Below: *Students changing classes.*

Honorary Degrees Conferred by Chaminade

Riley H. Allen
Editor, *Honolulu Star-Bulletin*

Vincent J. Moranz
Founder, Hawaiian Savings & Loan

The Honorable John A. Burns
Governor, State of Hawai'i

Walter F. Dillingham
President, Dillingham Corporation

Most Reverend James J. Sweeney, D.D.
Roman Catholic Bishop of Honolulu

Karl C. Lessbrick
President, Mauna Olu College

The Honorable Neal S. Blaisdell
Mayor, City and County of Honolulu

Clarence T.C. Ching
President, Loyalty Enterprises

George E. Freitas
President, Pacific Construction Company

Maurice J. Sullivan
President, Foodland Inc.

James W. Y. Wong
CPA, Owner, Small Business Investment Co.

The Honorable Daniel K. Inouye
United States Senator, Hawai'i

Mrs. Romalda Spalding
Author, Hawai'i Educator

Sr. Agnes Jerome Murphy, S.N.D.
Director, Special Education Center of Oahu

Peter T. Coleman
Deputy High Commissioner, Trust Territory of the Pacific Islands

Most Reverend John J. Scanlan, D.D.
Roman Catholic Bishop of Honolulu

Bro. Herman J. Gerber, S.M.
Registrar, Chaminade University

Bro. Oliver M. Aiu, S.M.
Teacher, Principal, President, Chancellor, Marianist Center of Hawai'i

Charles R. Borns
Professor of Business, Chaminade University

Henry A. Walker, Jr.
Chairman, Amfac, Inc.

The Rt. Rev. Edmond L. Browning
Bishop of the Episcopal Diocese of Hawai'i

Takuma Yamamoto
President, Fujitsu Limited

Rev. John Bolin, S.M.
Rector, Chaminade University

Edward K.O. Eu, R.M. KHS
Board of Governors, Board of Regents (Emeritus), Chaminade University

Bro. Raymond L. Fitz, S.M.
President, University of Dayton

Gary E. Liebl
Chairman of QLogic Corp. (ret.), Board of Regents, Chaminade University

Edward and Lynn Hogan
Founders, Pleasant Holidays, L.L.C.

The Honorable Daniel K. Akaka
United States Senator, Hawai'i

Ethics in Business Award Winners

These are occasional awards selected by Chaminade Master's degree candidates who research local companies seeking firms with a track record of ethical business practices and commitment to the community.

1993	Hilton Hawaiian Village
1994	Crazy Shirts Hawai'i
1995	AES Barbers Point, Inc.
1996	Aloha Airlines
1997	Foodland Supermarket, Ltd.
1998	Saturn of Honolulu
1999	Hard Rock Café, Honolulu
2000	Frito-Lay of Hawai'i
2001	Easter Seals of Hawai'i
2003	Outrigger Hotels, Hawai'i

Reverend John F. Bolin, S.M.

Fr. John Bolin has remained the thread of continuity and constancy at Chaminade, since he first arrived in Hawai'i in 1959. Today, as Senior Advisor to the President for Diocesan Relations, Fr. John provides wisdom, perspective, and a warm sense of humor. He has served in almost every capacity at the University, as well as holding the position of vicar general of the Diocese of Honolulu for six years, and leadership positions in Marianist provincial administration.

Fr. John was instrumental in the creation of the Marianist Center of Hawai'i. As Provincial of the Pacific Province from 1981 to 1989 in Cupertino, he was asked by then-president of Chaminade, Fr. Raymond Roesch, to clarify the governance relationship between Saint Louis School, Chaminade University and the Province. Fr. Bolin formed an Advisory Board, and, with the co-operation of the Boards of both schools, three corporations were formed, with the Province retaining ownership of the land and each school governing autonomously. Fr. Bolin returned to Hawai'i in 1989 and assumed the position of Vice-president for the Marianist Center of Hawai'i. He also holds the distinction of being the first Marianist to serve on the Chaminade Board of Regents.

Born in Brooklyn New York, Fr. John celebrated 60 years as a Marianist in 2004, and in May 2005 marked the 50th anniversary of his ordination as a priest. Fr. John has remarked on "how richly I have been blessed," but it is Chaminade that has been enriched with his good counsel and generous spirit. He has not only been a Chaminade professor, academic vice-president, rector, and Regent but has performed marriages and baptized many in the Chaminade 'ohana.

Fr. John will celebrate his 80th birthday on September 4, 2005.

Acknowledgements

While just three names appear on the dust jacket and the title page as the creators of this book, they represent a small percentage of the people who actually contributed.

I must first laud my two partners in this venture, Rector Bro. Jerry Bommer and English professor Linda Iwamoto. No one has ever been handed such willing, enthusiastic and talented accomplices!

My thanks also to regent Clif Kagawa for his role in this book.

The team at Chaminade was universally supportive, beginning at the top with President Sue taking us on a bouncy—and enlightening—golf cart tour of campus nooks and crannies. Many staff members—Kapono Ryan and Keith Kraughto especially—dug through old files on a mission to find priceless photographs. Kapono also arranged for three seminal figures, Fr. Stephen Tutas, Fr. David Schuyler and Bro. James Roberts, to tape long and fascinating interviews about the creation and growth of the University.

Other Chaminade people who proffered their help included Maile Alau, Marlene Baker, David Coleman, Valerie Coleman, Gary Cordova, Mike Fassiotto, Marites Fiesta, Bro. Robert Hoppe, Esther Ito, Be-Jay Kodama, Janine Kurosawa, Kahu John Keola Lake, Debbie Mellom, Larry Osborne, Sara Platte, Kekoa Simpson, Bro. Tom Spring, and William White.

And three Chaminade students willingly pitched in: Kim Chikazawa, Roseanne Malae and Jaren Maluyo.

Two members of the Saint Louis School 'ohana, Nola Ota and Timothy Los Banos provided valuable historical background.

In the world beyond Kalaepohaku, we were aided by Fr. Paul F. Vieson, S.M., Jennifer Gerth, and Kimberly Neuenschwander at the Marianist Archives in Dayton; Stephen J. Downes at *The Honolulu Advertiser*; Margaret Tippy and Briana Kaya at Tripler Army Medical Center; David Wilson at the National Personnel Records Center, St. Louis, MO; Mark Fujimoto at Professional Image in Mo'ili'ili; and Saint Louis grad and former English teacher Leon Mederios.

The tedious task of proofing the book—fact-by-fact, word-by-word, comma-by comma— was performed by Father John Bolin, Val Coleman, Gary Cordova, and Chaminade retirees Melba Kop, Loretta Petrie, and Jude Yablonsky. Still, any errors that slipped through are the creators' alone.

MS

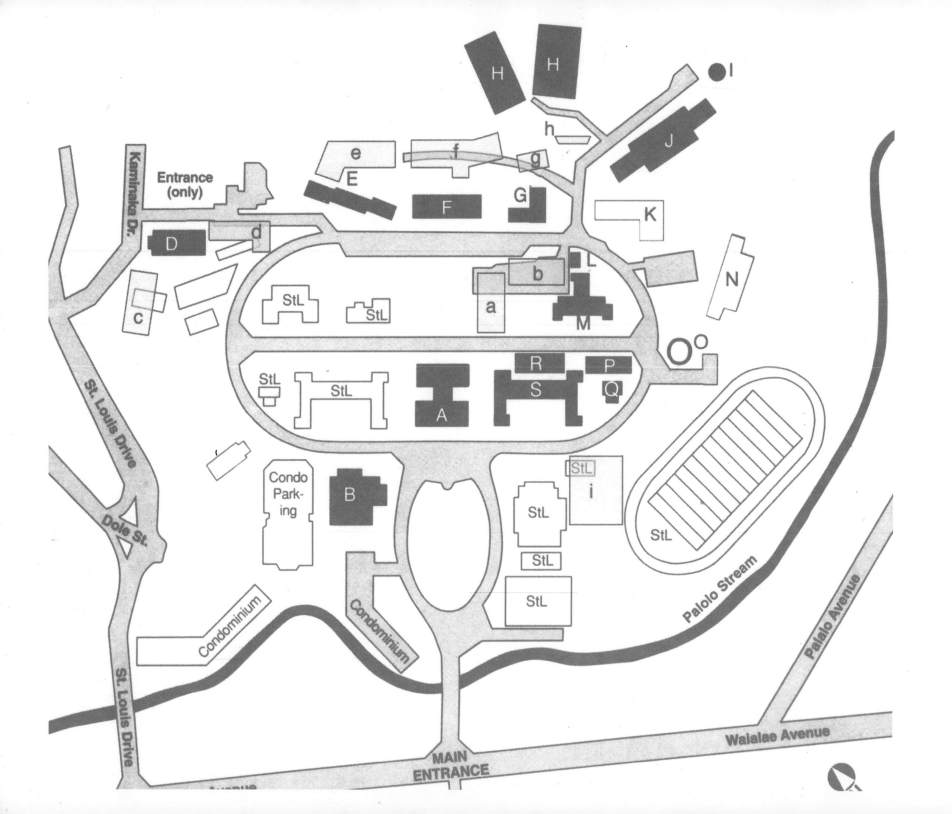

Speak Up, Tommy!

To Miky and all the hard-working dogs
who help to keep us safe – J.D.G.

For Nate and Jack – D.M.

Text copyright © 2012 by Jacqueline Dembar Greene
Illustrations copyright © 2012 Lerner Publishing Group, Inc.

KAR-BEN PUBLISHING, INC.
A division of Lerner Publishing Group, Inc.
241 First Avenue North
Minneapolis, MN 55401 U.S.A.
1-800-4-Karben

Website address: www.karben.com

Library of Congress Cataloging-in-Publication Data

Greene, Jacqueline Dembar.
     Speak up, Tommy! / by Jacqueline Dembar Greene ; illustrated by Deborah Melmon.
         p.   cm.
     Summary: Tommy, who recently moved to America from Israel, is teased because he
does not know English well and so does not speak loudly, but when a police officer visits
Tommy's class with a police dog that only understands Hebrew, friendship blooms.
     ISBN: 978-0-7613-7497-8 (lib. bdg : alk. paper)
     [1. Immigrants—Fiction. 2. Language and languages—Fiction. 3. Police—Fiction.
4. Police dogs—Fiction. 5. Human-animal communication—Fiction. 6. Jews—United
States—Fiction.]   I. Melmon, Deborah, ill. II. Title.
PZ7.G834Sp 2012
     [E]—dc23   2011029754

Manufactured in the United States of America

1 – BP – 7/15/12

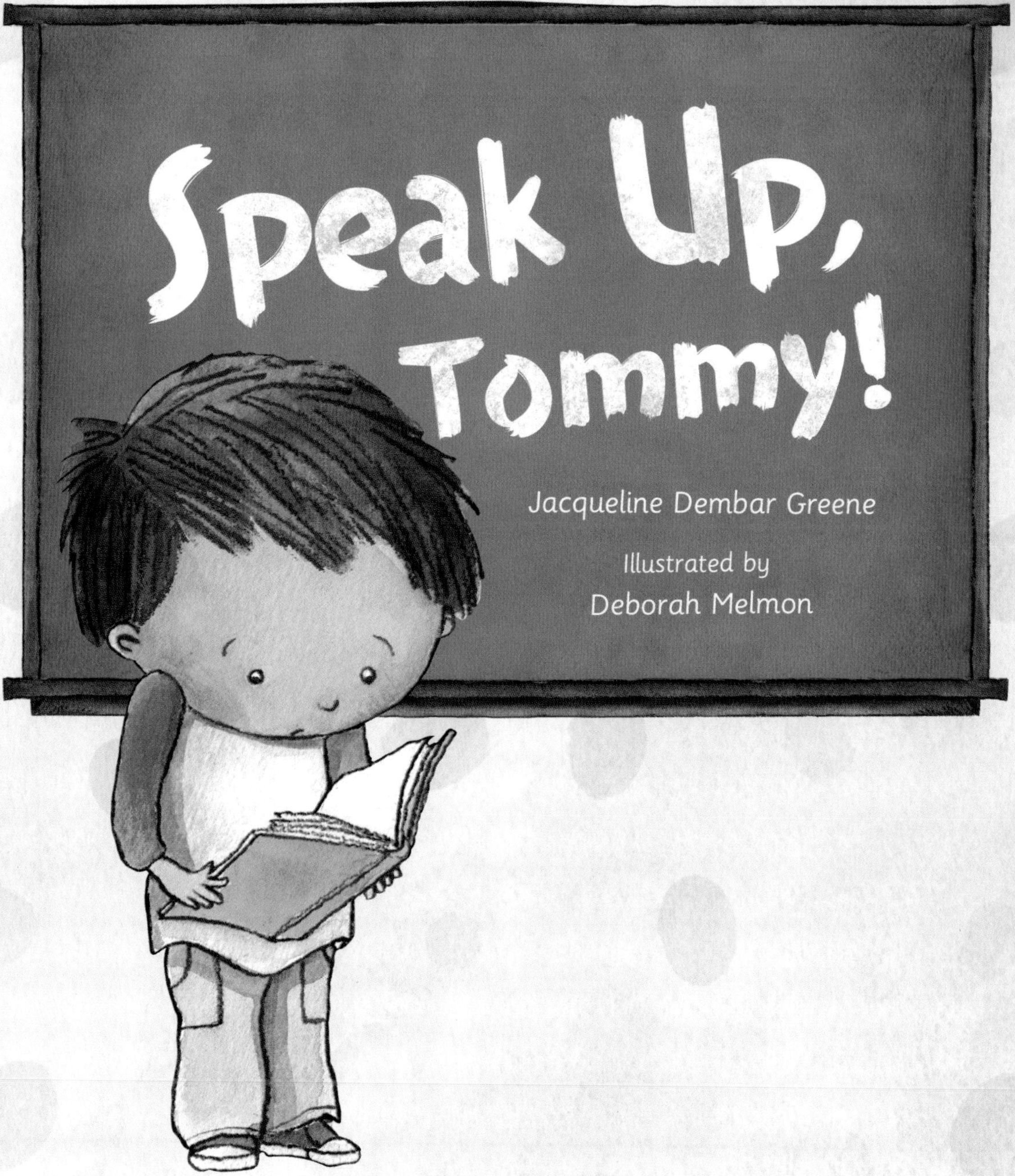

Speak Up, Tommy!

Jacqueline Dembar Greene

Illustrated by
Deborah Melmon

KAR-BEN
PUBLISHING

Tommy stayed by himself at recess, tossing a tennis ball against the school building.

"Do you know how to play football?" Charlie asked. "We're going to throw some passes."

Tommy was puzzled. "A football isn't to throw," he said. "A football is to kick."

Charlie laughed. "That's soccer!" he exclaimed.

Tommy was confused. When he lived in Israel his football was round. You kicked it down the field into the goal. "I don't know this American football game," he mumbled.

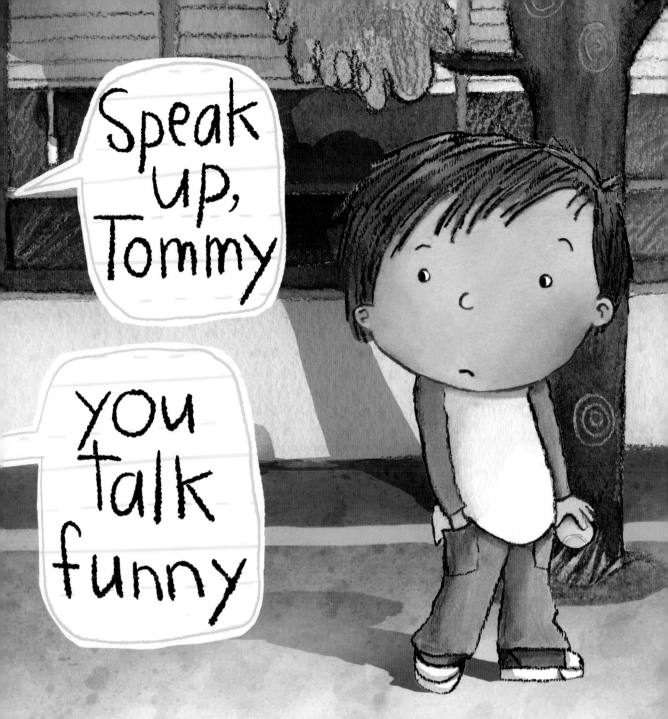

"Speak up, Tommy," teased Josh, imitating their teacher.

Charlie and Josh punched each other's arms and snickered. "You talk funny," said Charlie. Then they ran off.

Tommy's face grew hot. Why had he spoken English? The kids always teased him when he did. English words were hard to pronounce. In America, even his name had changed. In Israel his name was Tomer, which means "palm tree." He always stood taller when someone spoke his name. Now it was easier to be Tommy.

When it was time for reading circle, Tommy shrank down in his chair, trying to become invisible.

But Ms. Anderson called on him. "Would you begin, please, Tommy?"

There was nothing Tommy hated more than reading out loud, except having to read first. The words on the page swam in front of his eyes.

The 'r' sound rolled and trilled as he read. "Ron
likes to run," he whispered. "Ron races along."

"Speak up, Tommy," said Ms. Anderson. "We
can barely hear you." Some students giggled.

Ms. Anderson gave them a stern look. "Tommy's still learning English, and it's difficult at first. In this class we're a team, so let's cheer him on." She smiled at Tommy. "You're doing fine. But do speak up."

Tommy shook his head. He wouldn't speak English in school again.

After reading circle, Ms. Anderson gave Tommy a worksheet for tracing letters. They didn't look anything like Hebrew letters. He named each new letter in his head as he traced its shape. "A, B, C..." If only they looked more like *Aleph, Bet, and Gimel.*

"You're tracing letters?" Josh asked. "We did that in Kindergarten."

Tommy was glad when a knock on the door interrupted the teasing.

"As you know, we've been learning about our town," Ms. Anderson said, "and today we have special visitors from the Police Department."

The class had visited the Town Hall, the Post Office, and the Fire Station. Tommy liked field trips because he got to listen and didn't have to speak a word.

When Ms. Anderson opened the door, a man in a blue uniform walked in leading a frisky dog. "This is Officer Sweeney and his police dog Samson," she said.

Tommy's eyes opened wide. The Yellow Lab looked just like his dog Sabra who had to stay in Israel when his family moved. His grandparents were taking good care of her, but Tommy missed his dog every day.

Sniff
Sniff

"Sit," commanded Officer Sweeney. He pushed down on Samson's rump.

"When Samson was a puppy, he was chosen to become a special police dog," the officer explained. "He can smell things that people can't."

"My dog can smell a pizza box in a trash can," said Charlie.

Officer Sweeney grinned. "Not only can Samson smell food, but he's trained to smell things that could hurt people."

Tommy gasped. In Israel, police and dog teams helped to keep people safe. Samson must be one of those dogs!

"Police dogs work hard," said Officer Sweeney. "If Samson finds something suspicious, I reward him with a toy. He especially loves balls!"

Tommy fingered the tennis ball in his pocket, and suddenly Samson saw it and started to bark. Officer Sweeney whispered in the dog's ear, but Samson just gave him a puzzled look and kept barking. "Quiet!" said the officer.

QUIET!

Without warning, Samson pulled free and ran to Tommy, pawing at his pocket. The students laughed, and Tommy was glad that for once, they weren't laughing at him. Ms. Anderson rang her bell for silence.

With all the commotion, Tommy forgot that he didn't want to speak English out loud. In fact, he forgot to speak English at all. He could only think in Hebrew.

"Sheket!" he blurted out. Instantly, Samson stopped barking. He looked expectantly at Tommy.

"That's it!" Officer Sweeney exclaimed. "That's the Hebrew word for 'quiet.' I've been trying to say that, but Samson doesn't understand me."

The students looked at the police dog sitting quietly at Tommy's feet.

"Where did you learn to speak Hebrew?" Officer Sweeney asked.

"I'm from Israel," Tommy explained. "I speak Hebrew lots better than English." Officer Sweeney didn't laugh. And this time Charlie and Josh didn't laugh, either.

Officer Sweeney scratched his head.
"Samson was trained in Israel. I have a list
of Hebrew commands, but when I try to say
them, Samson ignores me." He chuckled.
"And he doesn't understand a word of
English!"

Ms. Anderson arched her eyebrows. "I think
you need to practice your Hebrew," she said.

The officer put his arm around Tommy's shoulder. "We could be a team," he said. "If you help me speak Hebrew, I'll help you with English."

"Neat!" Charlie exclaimed. "Tommy's going to train a police dog!"

Josh looked interested. "Maybe you could teach us Hebrew, too," he added.

Tommy found his voice. "Sure," he said, "if you teach me to play American football."

"It's a deal," Josh agreed.

Tommy held up the tennis ball. *"Shev,"* he said to Samson. "Sit."
The dog sat still as Tommy tossed the ball to Charlie. Then Charlie
hid it inside his desk.

"*Tavi,*" Tommy said. "Fetch." Samson trotted directly to the spot
where the ball was hidden and brought it to Tommy. Tommy
tossed it high in the air. "*Tafas!*" he commanded. "Catch!" The dog
caught the ball in mid air and dropped it at Tommy's feet.

"*Kelev tov!*" he praised him. And then he spoke up loud and clear.
"Good dog!"

Author's Note

Speak Up, Tommy! was inspired by a newspaper article about Sgt. John Fosket of the Helena, Montana Police Department, who was given a dog by an organization called Pups for Peace. The dog, Miky, was specially trained to sniff out hidden explosives and to sense someone acting suspiciously.

Sgt. Fosket had just one problem. Miky had been trained in Israel and only understood Hebrew commands.

The officer made himself flash cards with the Hebrew words, but had difficulty pronouncing them. Eventually, he enlisted the help of a Hasidic rabbi and a former member of the Israeli Defense Forces. Thanks to his Hebrew-speaking friends, the officer and the dog became a perfect team. They patrol the Montana Capitol building, and are sometimes called to investigate bomb threats.

English/Hebrew Dog Commands

Heel Ragli
Sit Shev
Stay He'asher
Down Artzah
Come Bo
Stand Amod

Fetch Tavi
Jump K'fotz
Go Out Hachutzah
Come Inside Kaness
Go Ahead Kadimah
Find Chapess
Guard Sh'mor
Let Go Azov
Eat Tochal
No Lo
Good Dog Kelev Tov
Quiet Sheket
Catch Tafas

Jacqueline Dembar Greene is the award-winning author of more than 30 books for young readers. Her books include the Rebecca Rubin series for American Girl, *The Secret Shofar of Barcelona*, and *Butchers and Bakers, Rabbis and Kings*, a finalist for the National Jewish Book Award. She lives in Wayland, Massachusetts.

Deborah Melmon has illustrated greeting cards, cookbooks, and children's books, as well as environmental art for the California Science Museum. She first realized she was going to be an artist when a paper-mache lion she created in seventh-grade art class was so large that it had to be driven home in the trunk of her parents' Oldsmobile with the lid up! Her previous books include *Picnic at Camp Shalom*. She graduated from the Academy of Art University in San Francisco and lives in Menlo Park, California with her dog.